MACHINE-EMBROIDERED QUILTS

Creating with Colorful Stitches

JENNIFER LOKEY

D1473247

Martingale®
& COMPANY

Credits

President   ◆   Nancy J. Martin
CEO   ◆   Daniel J. Martin
Publisher   ◆   Jane Hamada
Editorial Director   ◆   Mary V. Green
Managing Editor   ◆   Tina Cook
Technical Editor   ◆   Laurie Baker
Copy Editor   ◆   Ellen Balstad
Design Director   ◆   Stan Green
Illustrator   ◆   Laurel Strand
Cover and Text Designer   ◆   Trina Stahl
Photographer   ◆   Brent Kane

That Patchwork Place® is an imprint of Martingale & Company®.

Machine-Embroidered Quilts: Creating with Colorful Stitches
© 2004 by Jennifer Lokey

Martingale & Company
20205 144th Avenue NE
Woodinville, WA 98072-8478 USA
www.martingale-pub.com

Printed in China
09 08 07 06 05 04   8 7 6 5 4 3 2 1

Mission Statement

Dedicated to providing quality products and service to inspire creativity.

Library of Congress Cataloging-in-Publication Data

Lokey, Jennifer.
    Machine embroidered quilts / Jennifer Lokey.
      p. cm.
    ISBN 1-56477-516-X
   1. Patchwork—Patterns.   2. Quilting—Patterns.
  3. Embroidery, Machine—Patterns.   I. Title.
    TT835.L65 2004
    746.46—dc22

                          2003021717

Dedication

TO MY HUSBAND, Fred Lokey, my life partner on the journey. Your encouragement, confidence, and support have inspired me to continue to become all that I can.

Acknowledgments

FIRST AND FOREMOST, I thank God our Creator, who has given each of us the gift of creativity. For those of us who enjoy this kind of book, the gift takes expression in the shape of quilts. It seems to me that we are especially blessed.

To all my quilting friends over the years with whom I have shared the joy of quiltmaking, a big thank you. And particularly to my dearest aunt, Mary Jane Wilson, whose enthusiastic support I value as one of my greatest blessings.

I am most grateful to Betty Braud, whose friendship I treasure. She has always been available to bounce around ideas, listen, give input, and continually encourage. Betty pieced three of the quilts and quilted two of the wall quilts in this book with her beautiful workmanship. I appreciate the talents of Betty, as well as Beth Little, as experienced pattern writers. They were ready and willing to proof my first draft and give valuable feedback.

Allison Bayer of Allison's Machine Quilting in Plano, Texas, added her creative expertise and genuine gift of quilting interpretation to seven of the quilt projects in this book.

Sulky of America supplied much of the lovely rayon embroidery thread, and Isacord contributed the vibrant polyester embroidery thread, both of which made the digitized designs come alive with color.

The machine I used on the quilts in this book was the Brother Pacesetter ULT 2003 home embroidery and sewing machine. I want to thank the Brother Company and say that the Pacesetter has performed beautifully.

Thank you to Oklahoma Embroidery Supply and Design, Cactus Punch, Amazing Designs, and Zundt Design for the quality digitized designs that inspired the quilts in this book.

And last, thank you to Mary Green, Karen Soltys, and the staff at Martingale & Company for their belief in the concept of this book. I admire and respect the quality publications that they provide to the quilting community and am pleased to be a contributor.

CONTENTS

INTRODUCTION

Ｄ ESIGN IDEAS TUMBLE around in my head all the time. Sometimes it is wonderfully fun just to envision the endless possibilities. Sometimes it is frustrating because I don't have the time to devote to extracting them. And sometimes it is greatly rewarding to see an idea come to fruition and be able to share it with others. This book is one of those rewarding times.

Quilt designing and publishing were my love and my living for 15 years as cofounder and president of Four Corners Designs. In April of 2001, I left Four Corners in the capable hands of Karen Roossein and ventured out on my own to focus more on designing.

For some time now, I have observed the growing popularity of embroidery machines for the home sewer. These machines are capable of executing beautiful embroidery designs, but the focus for these designs is often on clothing and accessories.

It seems to me that the combination of fabric piecing and digitized embroidery designs is the next innovative step in the world of quilts. Marvelous quilts that feature free-motion machine embroidery, a form of painting with stitches, are something I have observed recently. These quilts are truly lovely, but the technique does take practice to master. Digitized embroidery designs are as easy as pushing a button and threading a needle—something anyone can do!

However, many quilters have purchased machines with this exciting capability and have yet to enjoy all the project potential. The purpose of this book is to inspire and encourage quilters who own an embroidery machine to incorporate digitized embroidery designs into their quilts when the quilt design calls for that special addition. The creative process can start with the digitized design, a favorite quilt block, or a particularly inspiring piece of fabric. Just think, any quilt with an alternate block is a natural consideration for a machine-embroidered design. Fill it with an embroidered picture, a classic design element such as lace, or a special phrase. There are actual digitized quilt block designs that may enhance your pieced creation when thread colors are chosen to coordinate. Coordinate the themes and colors, and you are ready to go. Then consider the possibility of creating your own digitized designs with one of the software packages available today. Once you get started, the ideas will soon be tumbling out. Isn't this fun?

If you don't have a machine with embroidery capabilities or you want to use another embellishment method, most of the quilt projects provide an alternative to use in place of the digitized design. There's something here for everyone to enjoy!

GENERAL INSTRUCTIONS

No matter how you choose to embellish your project, you will find the basics for each application in this section. If machine embroidery is your preferred method, be sure to consult with your sewing-machine dealer if you are unfamiliar with how to use the embroidery functions on your machine.

MACHINE-EMBROIDERY BASICS

To create the very best sewn designs, there are some important machine-embroidery terms you will need to understand, supplies you will need to have on hand, and techniques you will need to implement.

♦   **Copyright:** Copyright issues are an important part of the embroidery world. We all want to enjoy the benefits of this art form and therefore it is important to understand the rights we have and those we do not have. You may sew a design you have purchased from a commercial design company on as many garments and quilts as you wish, as often as you wish, unless otherwise stated on the design card information. Design cards purchased from a machine dealer usually have additional copyright information on them. When cards state that the designs included are licensed, it means that the designs may not be sold as sewn products and may be used only for personal use by the original purchaser. You may not sell, trade, copy, loan, transfer, or in any way duplicate the design software purchased as design cards, disks, or downloaded files—in any part, or as a whole—without violating copyright law. For more information, visit www.embroidery-protection.org.

♦   **Digitized Designs:** This term refers to the programmed stitch patterns that tell the computer within the embroidery machine how to sew a specific picture. Designs are available in many different formats. Most home embroidery machines have designs programmed into the machine or on cards or disks that fit into the machine. These are perfect to use as motifs in a quilt design. An endless variety of designs on embroidery cards or computer disks can be purchased from a machine dealer and many may be downloaded from the Internet for a fee or for free. Check "Resources" on page 77 for suppliers who carry the digitized designs used in this book, as well as many others.

Downloading designs is an easy operation. Be sure to request the correct file format for your specific machine. (Check with the manufacturer for the format. For example, the format for a Brother machine is PES.) There are two precautions you should consider as you download any files from the Internet: (1) Be sure you know where a design came from before you download it so that you don't unintentionally download a copyrighted design. (2) Always protect your computer with a virus-scan program that can be updated frequently.

♦ **Fabric:** Because all of the projects in this book are quilts or quilt related, the instructions assume you will be embroidering on high-quality, 100%-cotton fabric. Do not use lightweight cotton such as batiste.

♦ **Hoops:** Each home embroidery machine comes with a hoop specifically designed for it. Some machines have two or three hoops in graduating sizes. The hoop is made up of two parts: the inner hoop and the outer hoop. The outer hoop attaches to the machine and the inner hoop firmly holds the stabilizer and fabric within the outer hoop.

How you hoop the fabric is one of the most important aspects of machine embroidery. Incorrect hooping can cause distorted designs and puckered fabric, so be sure you understand the proper way to use your hoops. In general, to hoop your fabric, place the chosen stabilizer on the wrong side of the fabric. You can keep the layers from shifting by temporarily bonding the fabric and stabilizer together with a temporary spray adhesive, if desired. Loosen the screw on the outer hoop and place the hoop on a stable, flat surface. Place the stabilized fabric over the outer hoop, fabric side up. Press the inner hoop into position over the fabric so that the fabric is smooth and taut. Tighten the screw to hold it in place.

♦ **Machine Needles:** For most projects, size 80/12 universal needles work very well if you are using a quilting-weight cotton fabric and 40-weight rayon thread. You may need a different type or size of needle if you use a different fabric weight or type of thread other than that suggested for the project.

♦ **Scissors:** Quality embroidery scissors are an essential tool for accurate trimming. There are a variety of types to choose from and your choice depends on personal preference. My favorite style is a small scissor with a curved, sharp blade that enables me to clip threads close to the surface without damaging the embroidery with the scissor tips.

♦ **Stabilizer:** Stabilizer is the backing used to give a good foundation to the design being sewn. There are many types available, but for woven fabrics such as cotton, a tear-away stabilizer works well. Tear-away stabilizer is available in several weights and comes in black or white to coordinate with any fabric. Remove it from the final embroidery by gently tearing it away from the stitched design. Before you begin a project, find the stabilizer weight that is best for the project by test-sewing on several with the fabrics and threads you will use in the project.

♦ **Test Sew-Out:** Always make a sample of the design you have chosen, using the same fabric, stabilizer, and threads that you will use in the actual project. It is better to make changes on a sample than to have to rip out stitches on your quilt block.

♦ **Thread:** Create quality embroidery designs with 40-weight rayon or polyester embroidery thread in the needle. The bobbin thread should be 60-weight polyester especially designed for machine embroidery. Needle and bobbin threads are both available in a wide variety of colors.

Appliqué Basics

Several of the projects in this book give the option to substitute an appliqué design in place of the digitized machine embroidery. I used fusible-web appliqué for the alternative technique blocks shown. It is quick and easy, and the edges may be finished with a decorative hand or machine stitch. Basic instructions for hand appliqué with the freezer-paper method are included for those who enjoy a slower pace and a beautifully finished look.

Making Templates

For both fusible-web appliqué and freezer-paper appliqué you will need to begin by making a template for each appliqué piece. The appliqué patterns are provided with each project. Each shape is numbered. Trace the exact outline of each shape onto transparent template plastic with a fine-tip permanent marking pen. *Do not add seam allowances.* Carefully cut out each template on the traced line.

Fusible-Web Appliqué

Fusible web allows you to permanently adhere the appliqué shapes to the background fabric and leave the edges unfinished or embellish them with hand or machine stitching. Follow the manufacturer's instructions for fusing because each brand is slightly different.

1. Place the paper-backed fusible web over the appliqué shape, paper side up. Using a pencil, trace around each shape. Leave 1" of space between each shape. Cut out each shape, leaving ½" around all edges.

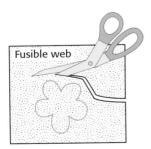

2. Follow the manufacturer's instructions to fuse each cut shape to the wrong side of the appropriate fabric.

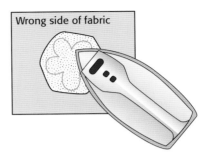

3. Cut out each appliqué shape on the drawn line.

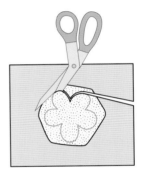

4. Peel away the paper backing and place the shape in position on the background fabric. When you are satisfied with the placement, fuse it in place.

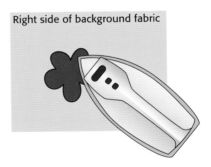

5. You can finish the edges by hand or machine. The satin and buttonhole stitches are two attractive machine-finishing stitch selections. A handmade blanket stitch adds a nice texture to the appliqué edge (refer to "Hand-Embroidery Stitches" on page 14).

Freezer-Paper Appliqué

Freezer paper is coated on one side and will temporarily stick to fabric when heat is applied. Using this method helps maintain a clean, crisp shape for hand appliqué.

1. Place the template on the noncoated (dull) side of the freezer paper and trace around the shape with a sharp pencil.

2. Cut out the traced shape on the drawn line. Do not add seam allowance.

3. Lay the freezer-paper shape, coated (shiny) side down, on the wrong side of the appropriate fabric. Iron the shape in place with a hot, dry iron.

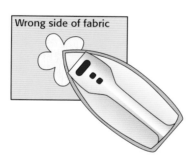

4. Cut around the freezer paper shape, adding a generous ¼" seam allowance around the paper shape as you cut.

5. Turn the seam allowance over the edge of the freezer paper and hand baste it in place with contrasting thread.

6. Pin the prepared appliqué shape in place on the background fabric. Refer to "Traditional Appliqué Stitch" on page 13 to stitch the shape in place.

7. Remove the basting stitches. Then remove the freezer paper from the wrong side by making a small slit in the background fabric behind the appliqué and gently pulling the paper out with a pair of tweezers.

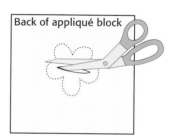

YO-YO EMBELLISHMENT

A yo-yo is a fabric embellishment that I love to use to add dimension to a quilt. Two of the quilts in this book, "Flowers in a Basket" (page 40) and "Floral Wreath" (page 63), suggest the use of yo-yos in the alternative technique block.

To make a yo-yo, follow these steps:
1. Trace the circle pattern given with the project onto template plastic or heavy cardboard. Use the template to trace the required number of circles onto the wrong side of the appropriate fabric(s). Cut out the circles.

Traditional Appliqué Stitch

The traditional appliqué stitch, or blind stitch, produces the illusion of design shapes floating on the surface of the background fabric. The objective is to hide your stitches.

1. Choose a thread color that matches the appliqué fabric. Cut a single strand, 18" to 20" long. Thread your appliqué needle and knot one end of the thread.

2. Begin the first stitch by placing the needle point underneath the appliqué shape only, not the background fabric. Bring the needle out through the seam fold line and pull so that the knot is hidden in the seam allowance.

3. Insert the needle tip into the background fabric precisely where the thread came out of the folded edge of the appliqué fabric. With a continuous motion, bring the needle up through the very edge of the folded appliqué approximately ⅛" away from the last stitch point. Pull the thread all the way through and gently snug the stitch in place. Continue around the entire appliqué shape.

Appliqué Stitch

4. To end your stitching, insert your needle into the background fabric and bring the thread to the wrong side. Take two or three stitches behind the appliqué shape and knot the thread.

2. With the fabric circle wrong side up, fold the raw edge toward the center a scant ¼". Using a single strand of sturdy quilting thread, insert the needle through the folded fabric from the side that is facing up. Take ⅛"- to ¼"-long stitches all the way around the outer folded edge of the circle.

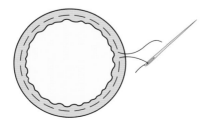

3. When you reach the point where you began, pull the gathering thread to close the circle. Flatten the circle so that the gathers meet in the center. Take several stitches to tie off and secure the gathers.

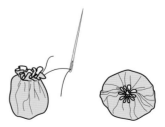

4. Appliqué the yo-yo in place with the gathered side up.

HAND-EMBROIDERY BASICS

SEVERAL OF the quilts in this book offer hand embroidery as a lovely alternative to machine embroidery. Transfer the design to the background fabric and bring it to life with one or two of the simple embroidery stitches described at right.

To transfer and embroider the design, follow these steps:

1. Trace the design onto tracing paper with a fine-point permanent marker. Center the background fabric, right side up, over the traced design. Trace the design onto the fabric with a fine-point permanent marker such as Pigma or Gelly Roll, in a color close to the chosen thread color. A light box may be used for tracing onto darker fabrics. If you do not have a light box, tape the traced design to a window pane (obviously during daylight), tape the fabric over the design, and trace.

2. Place the background fabric in an embroidery hoop with the design centered. Thread an embroidery needle with two strands of embroidery floss or one strand of pearl cotton. Knot one end of the strand(s). Bring the needle up from the back of the fabric and work the desired stitch (refer to "Hand-Embroidery Stitches" at right). To finish, weave the end of the thread back through one or two stitches on the wrong side.

3. When the embroidery is complete, place the piece over a towel and press gently on the wrong side to remove the embroidery hoop creases.

4. Refer to "Trimming the Embellished Pieces" on page 15 to prepare the design for inclusion in the quilt.

HAND-EMBROIDERY STITCHES

Blanket Stitch
Use this stitch to finish the edges of fused appliqué shapes. It will add decorative appeal and hold the appliqué securely in place.

Satin Stitch
Satin stitches lie side by side, just touching. They are used to fill open areas.

Stem Stitch
When sewing stem stitches, keep the thread either above the line for a convex curve or below the line for a concave curve.

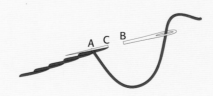

TRIMMING THE EMBELLISHED PIECES

THE EMBELLISHED blocks are cut larger than needed to make the embellishing process easier. After they are complete, they must be cut to the correct size in order to fit into the project. To trim the pieces evenly, follow the steps below. All of the projects follow these instructions, with the exception of "Flowers in a Basket" (page 40) and "Garden Stepping-Stones" (page 46). The trimming instructions for these quilts are included with the project instructions.

1. Press the embellished piece from the wrong side.

2. To determine the center of the embellished design, measure the length of the design and divide by 2. Place a pin at the center point. For example, if the total length of the design is 2⅝", place a pin at the 1 5/16" point. Measure the width of the design, in line with the length pin, and place a pin at the center point. For example, if the total width of the design is 2½", place a pin at the 1¼" point. The point at which the length and width centers intersect is the center of the design.

3. The instructions for each quilt project will note the measurement for the trimmed piece. Divide this measurement by 2. For example, if the trimmed size is 4½" square, the divided measurement would be 2¼". From the center point of the trimmed piece, measure out 2¼" in all four directions and draw light pencil lines for trimming. Cut out the block on the drawn lines.

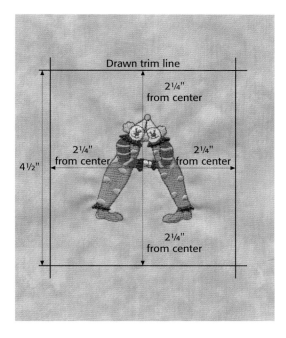

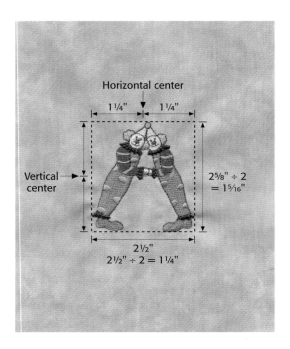

FROM ME TO YOU

By Jennifer Lokey, 23" x 27". Quilted by Betty Braud.

This joyful little wall quilt was my very first project incorporating machine embroidery with traditional quilt piecing. I had no preconceived ideas about this quilt—it was the result of a class that I took on the Viking Designer I embroidery/ sewing machine. The choice was mine as to the embroidery design to practice stitch. The free-form daisies appealed to me and I was pleased with the sewn sample that I took home. My next thought was what should I do with this delightful piece? It called for a bright, cheerful fabric combination and, as you can see, the embroidery and fabric complement each other wonderfully.

MATERIALS

Yardage is based on 42"-wide fabric.

For the machine-embroidered project:

- ⅞ yard of multicolor floral print for third and fifth borders
- ½ yard of diagonally printed, multicolor stripe for second border and binding
- ½ yard of pink solid for third and fourth borders
- ⅜ yard of white solid for center design background
- ⅛ yard of yellow tone-on-tone for first border
- ⅞ yard of fabric for backing
- 27" x 31" piece of batting
- Digitized embroidery design of your choice that stitches out to approximately 6" x 10". The daisy bouquet design on the featured project is "built in" (integrated into the software of the machine) to the Viking Designer I. It is from the Design I Sampler, design 1. This design requires a larger hoop format. Any design you choose of approximately the same size will work nicely.
- Tear-away stabilizer
- Robison-Anton 40-weight rayon embroidery threads: Scarlet Red (2219), Meadow Green

APPLIQUÉ ALTERNATIVE

The alternative design features bright bursts of appliquéd flowers that are equally as charming as their stitched counterparts.

(2226), Begonia Pink (2228), Cornsilk Gold (2395), Sienna Brown (2402), Wicker Brown (2489)

For the alternative appliquéd design:
You will need the fabrics and batting listed for the embroidered project, as well as the following:

- 5" x 5" square *each* of 4 assorted bright fabrics for daisy blossom appliqués (patterns 5, 7, 9, and 11)
- 5" x 9" rectangle of green print for stem appliqués (patterns 1, 2, 3, and 4)
- 5" x 5" square of brown print for flower center appliqués (patterns 6, 8, 10, and 12)
- Freezer paper or fusible web, depending on the appliqué method used
- Threads for finishing appliqué edges (optional)

CUTTING

All measurements include ¼"-wide seam allowances.

From the white solid, cut:
- 1 rectangle, 10" x 14"

From the yellow tone-on-tone, cut:
- 2 strips, 1" x 42"; crosscut the strips into:
  - 2 strips, 1" x 12½"
  - 2 strips, 1" x 9½"

From the multicolor stripe, cut:
- 2 strips, 2" x 42"; crosscut the strips into:
  - 2 strips, 2" x 13½"
  - 2 strips, 2" x 12½"
- 3 strips, 2½" x 42"

From the pink solid, cut:
- 1 rectangle, 8" x 24"
- 3 strips, 1" x 42"

From the multicolor floral, cut:
- 1 rectangle, 8" x 24"
- 4 squares, 2½" x 2½"
- 4 strips, 3½" x 42"

ASSEMBLING THE QUILT TOP

1. Machine embroider or appliqué the 10" x 14" white rectangle with the daisy design. If you choose to machine embroider, refer to "Machine-Embroidery Basics" on page 9.

   If you choose to appliqué, refer to "Appliqué Basics" on page 11 to prepare and cut the appliqués from the appropriate fabrics, using the patterns on page 20. Trace and cut out one *each* of appliqué patterns 1–12.

2. Refer to "Trimming the Embellished Pieces" on page 15 to trim the embellished block to 8½" x 12½".

3. To add the first and second borders, stitch the 1" x 12½" yellow strips to the sides of the embellished rectangle. Press the seams toward the strips. Stitch the 1" x 9½" yellow strips to the top and bottom edges of the embellished rectangle. Press the seams toward the strips. Repeat to stitch the 2" x 13½" strips of multicolor stripe to the sides of the quilt top and then the 2" x 12½" strips of multicolor stripe to the top and bottom edges of the quilt top. Press the seams toward the newly added strips after each addition.

   NOTE: *Be sure to cut the first and second border strips to the lengths listed so that the pieced third border will fit.*

4. To make the half-square-triangle units for the third border, use a pencil or water-soluble marker to draw two rows of seven 2⅞" squares each on the wrong side of the 8" x 24" floral-print rectangle, leaving no space between the squares and rows as shown. Draw a diagonal line through each square. Place the marked rectangle right sides together with the 8" x 24" pink rectangle. Pin the layers together between the diagonal lines. Sew ¼" from both sides of each diagonal line.

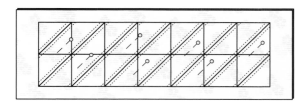

5. Cut along each diagonal, vertical, and horizontal line. This will yield 28 half-square-triangle units. Open each unit and press the seam toward the pink fabric. Cut away the extended corners.

6. Stitch eight half-square-triangle units together as shown to make a side border strip. Make 2. Stitch six half-square-triangle units together as shown to make the top and bottom borders. Make 2. Press the seams for each border strip in one direction.

Top and Bottom Borders
Make 2.

Side Borders
Make 2.

7. Stitch the pieced side borders to the quilt top as shown. Press the seams toward the second border. Sew a 2½" floral-print square to each end of the top and bottom border strips. Press the seams toward the squares. Stitch the top and bottom border strips to the top and bottom edges of the quilt top. Press the seams toward the second border.

8. Refer to "Adding Borders" on page 71 to measure the quilt top for borders. Cut the 1" x 42" pink strips to the correct lengths and stitch them to the quilt top. Repeat with the 3½" x 42" floral-print strips.

FINISHING

REFER TO "Quilt Finishing" on pages 71–75.

1. Layer the quilt top with batting and backing; baste.

2. Quilt as desired. The featured project was quilted along all of the seam lines. The embroidered design was outlined.

3. Trim the backing and batting even with the quilt top.

4. Bind the quilt with the 2½" x 42" multicolor stripe strips.

5. Add a label.

**Alternative Block
Appliqué Patterns**

A TOUCH OF LACE

By Jennifer Lokey, 54" x 54". Quilted by Allison Bayer.

Geometric designs intrigue me. That is one of the many reasons I enjoy the art of quilting. Curves can certainly enhance a geometric design, and I feel that this quilt illustrates that. The lovely digitized circular lace pattern in this diagonal arrangement complements the squares and triangles that make up the rest of the design.

MATERIALS

Yardage is based on 42"-wide fabric.

For the machine-embroidered project:
♦   1½ yards of green print for blocks and outer border
♦   1⅛ yards of red floral print for blocks
♦   ¾ yard of small red print for inner border and binding
♦   ¾ yard of taupe floral print for blocks
♦   ⅝ yard of beige fabric for embellished blocks
♦   3½ yards of fabric for backing
♦   58" x 58" square of batting
♦   Digitized embroidery design of your choice that stitches out to approximately 3¾" x 3¾". The lace design used in the featured project is from Oklahoma Embroidery Supply and Design, design NX964.
♦   Tear-away stabilizer
♦   Two large spools (850 yards) of Sulky Bayberry Red (1169) 40-weight rayon embroidery thread

For the alternative appliquéd design:
You will need the fabrics and batting listed for the machine-embroidered project, as well as the following:
♦   ⅞ yard of red print for appliqués
♦   Freezer paper or fusible web, depending on the appliqué method used
♦   Thread for finishing appliqué edges (optional)

DESIGN ALTERNATIVES

Substitute either the appliqué design or the hand-embroidery pattern if one offers a more appealing alternative to the machine-embroidered design.

For the alternative hand-embroidered design:
You will need the fabrics and batting listed for the machine-embroidered project, as well as the following:
♦   Two skeins of DMC Red Fruit (816) 6-strand embroidery floss
♦   Hand-embroidery needle

CUTTING

All measurements include ¼"-wide seam allowances.

From the beige fabric, cut:
♦   2 strips, 8" x 42"; crosscut the strips into 9 squares, 8" x 8"

From the red floral print, cut:
- 3 strips, 3⅛" x 42"; crosscut the strips into 36 squares, 3⅛" x 3⅛". Cut each square in half once diagonally to yield 72 triangles.
- 8 strips, 2¾" x 42"; crosscut 4 strips into:
    8 rectangles, 2¾" x 9½"
    16 squares, 2¾" x 2¾"

From the green print, cut:
- 7 strips, 2¾" x 42"; crosscut 3 strips into 36 squares, 2¾" x 2¾"
- 6 strips, 4" x 42"

From the taupe floral print, cut:
- 4 strips, 5" x 42"; crosscut the strips into:
    4 rectangles, 5" x 9½"
    24 squares, 5" x 5"

From the small red print, cut:
- 5 strips, 1½" x 42"
- 6 strips, 2½" x 42"

MAKING THE BLOCKS

1. To make the embellished blocks, machine embroider, appliqué, or hand embroider the 8" x 8" beige squares with the chosen design. If you choose to machine embroider, refer to "Machine-Embroidery Basics" on page 9.

    If you choose to appliqué, refer to "Appliqué Basics" on page 11 to prepare and cut the appliqués from the red fabric, using the patterns on page 26. Trace and cut out nine *each* of appliqué patterns 1–9.

    If you choose to hand embroider, use the pattern on page 26 and refer to "Hand-Embroidery Basics" on page 14 to satin stitch the dots and stem stitch the remaining lines of the design with the red embroidery floss.

2. Refer to "Trimming the Embellished Pieces" on page 15 to trim the embellished squares to 7" x 7".

3. Stitch a red triangle to two adjacent sides of each green square as shown. Press the seams toward the triangles. Make 36 corner units.

Make 36.

4. Sew a corner unit to each side of each embellished square, stitching opposite sides first. Press the seams toward the corner units. Make nine embellished blocks. The blocks should measure 9½" x 9½".

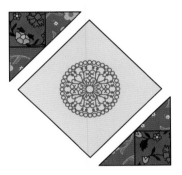

Make 9.

5. To make the alternate blocks, draw a diagonal line from corner to corner on the wrong side of 16 red floral squares. Place a square on opposite corners of each taupe floral rectangle. Sew on the marked line; trim ¼" from the stitching line and press the seam toward the triangle corner. Repeat with the opposite two corners. Make four units.

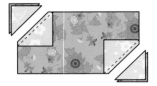 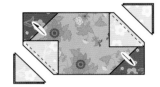

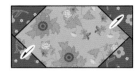

6. Stitch a red floral rectangle to each long side of each unit from step 5 as shown. Make four alternate blocks. The blocks should measure 9½" x 9½".

 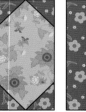 

Make 4.

7. To make the Four Patch blocks, join each of the remaining 2¾" x 42" green print strips to a remaining 2¾" x 42" red floral strip along the long edges to make a strip set. Make four. The strip sets should measure 5" wide when sewn. Crosscut the strips into 48 segments, 2¾" wide.

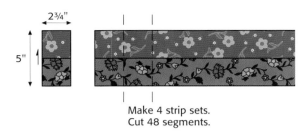

Make 4 strip sets.
Cut 48 segments.

8. Stitch two segments from step 7 together to make a four-patch unit. Make 24.

Make 24.

9. Join the four-patch units and the taupe floral squares as shown to make four of Four Patch A block and eight of Four Patch B block. Be careful to place the four-patch units exactly as shown. The blocks should measure 9½" x 9½".

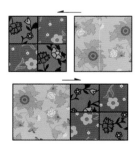 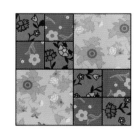

Four Patch A
Make 4.

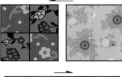 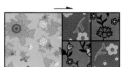 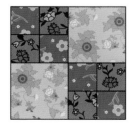

Four Patch B
Make 8.

ASSEMBLING THE QUILT TOP

1. Arrange the embellished blocks, the alternate blocks, and the Four Patch blocks into five horizontal rows of five blocks each as shown, placing the Four Patch A blocks in the quilt-top corners. Be careful to place all of the Four Patch and alternate blocks exactly as shown. Sew the blocks in each row together, and then join the rows to complete the center quilt design.

2. Refer to "Adding Borders" on page 71 to cut the 1½" x 42" small red print strips to the correct lengths for the inner border; stitch them to the quilt top. Repeat with the 4" x 42" green print strips for the outer border.

FINISHING

REFER TO "Quilt Finishing" on pages 71–75.

1. Layer the quilt top with batting and backing; baste.

2. Quilt as desired. The embellished blocks in the featured quilt are accentuated with four concentric circles of quilting. The remaining pieced blocks are crosshatched diagonally every 1½". The outer border features a feather-style design.

3. Trim the backing and batting even with the quilt top.

4. Bind the quilt with the 2½" x 42" small red print strips.

5. Add a label.

**Alternative Block
Appliqué Patterns**

1

2

3

4

5

6

7

8

9

**Alternative Block
Hand-Embroidery Pattern**

A TO Z, COME PLAY WITH ME

By Jennifer Lokey, 44" x 56". Quilted by Allison Bayer.

I have grandchildren and am a child at heart myself—I couldn't resist these animated little clowns, twisting and turning to shape this playful alphabet. The twenty-six machine-embroidered clowns accent larger appliquéd blocks with more clown motifs.

MATERIALS

Yardage is based on 42"-wide fabric.

For the machine-embroidered project:

- 2 yards of lavender fabric for embellished blocks and small appliqué blocks
- 1¼ yards of blue print for half-square-triangle units, large appliqué blocks, appliqués, outer border, and binding
- ⅞ yard of yellow check for large appliqué blocks and half-square-triangle units
- ⅝ yard of yellow dot print for strip sets and inner border
- ½ yard of light green print for strip sets and appliqués
- ⅜ yard of pink-and-orange stripe for appliqués and strip sets
- ¼ yard *each* of 2 red prints for large appliqué blocks and appliqués
- ¼ yard of medium green print for large appliqué blocks and appliqués
- 3 yards of fabric for backing
- 48" x 60" rectangle of batting
- Digitized embroidery designs of your choice that stitch out to approximately 2¾" x 2¾". The clown alphabet designs used in the featured quilt are from Amazing Designs, Design Collection AD1277.
- Tear-away stabilizer
- Sulky 40-weight rayon embroidery threads: Red (561), Yellow (1023), Goldenrod (1024), Medium Blue (1029), Pale Peach (1064), Emerald Green (1079), Ecru (1082),

APPLIQUÉ ALTERNATIVE

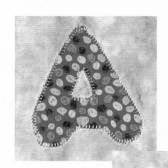

Traditional letter patterns are given if you prefer to appliqué the alphabet shapes rather than machine embroider them.

Brown (1129), Fuchsia (1192), Gray (1219), Bright Pink (1224), Salmon Peach (1259), Lime Green (1510), Deep Rose (1511), Light Rose (1533), Team Blue (1535)
- Freezer paper or fusible web, depending on the appliqué method used

For the alternative appliquéd design:
You will need the fabrics and batting listed for the embroidered project, as well as the following:
- ⅛ yard extra of each appliqué fabric listed to use for alphabet appliqués
- Freezer paper or fusible web, depending on the appliqué method used

CUTTING

All measurements include ¼"-wide seam allowances.

From the lavender fabric, cut:
- 6 strips, 9" x 42"; crosscut the strips into 26 rectangles, 8" x 9"
- 3 squares, 5½" x 5½"

From the yellow check, cut:
- 2 strips, 4⅞" x 42"; crosscut the strips into 12 squares, 4⅞" x 4⅞". Cut each square in half once diagonally to yield 24 triangles.
- 2 strips, 7¼" x 42"; crosscut the strips into 6 squares, 7¼" x 7¼"

From *each* of the 2 red prints and the medium green print, cut:
- 1 strip, 4⅞" x 42" (3 strips total); crosscut *each* strip into 6 squares (18 total), 4⅞" x 4⅞". Cut each square in half once diagonally to yield 12 triangles (36 total).

From the blue print, cut:
- 1 strip, 4⅞" x 42"; crosscut the strip into 6 squares, 4⅞" x 4⅞". Cut each square in half once diagonally to yield 12 triangles.
- 5 strips, 3½" x 42"
- 6 strips, 2½" x 42"

From the light green print, cut:
- 6 strips, 1½" x 42"

From the yellow dot print, cut:
- 11 strips, 1½" x 42"

From the pink-and-orange stripe, cut:
- 2 strips, 2½" x 42"; crosscut the strips into 14 rectangles, 2½" x 4½"

MAKING THE BLOCKS AND UNITS

1. To make the embellished blocks, machine embroider or appliqué each lavender 8" x 9" rectangle with the chosen design. If you choose to machine embroider, refer to "Machine-Embroidery Basics" on page 9.

   If you choose to appliqué, refer to "Appliqué Basics" on page 11 to prepare and cut the appliqués from the appropriate fabrics, using the patterns on page 31. Enlarge the pattern to the percentage indicated, and then trace and cut out one *each* of appliqués A–Z.

2. Refer to "Trimming the Embellished Pieces" on page 15 to trim each embellished rectangle to 4½" x 4½".

3. To make the large appliqué blocks, refer to "Appliqué Basics" on page 11 to prepare and cut the appliqués from the appropriate fabrics, using the patterns on page 32. Refer to the quilt photo for fabric placement, if necessary. Prepare and cut out one *each* of appliqués 1–4 and two *each* of appliqués 5–11.

4. Center one hat, shoe, or flower appliqué on each on-point 7¼" yellow check square; appliqué the shapes in place. Trim each square to 6¼" x 6¼", keeping the design centered. Randomly stitch a red, green, or blue triangle to each side of each appliquéd square, stitching opposite sides first. Press the seams toward the triangles.

Make 6 total.

5. To make the small appliqué blocks, prepare and cut out three *each* of appliqués 12–14 on page 32. Center each ball shape on a 5½" lavender square and appliqué in place. Trim each square to 4½" x 4½", keeping the design centered.

Make 3.

6. To make the half-square-triangle units, sew a yellow check triangle to each of the remaining red, blue, and medium green triangles. Make 24 total.

Make 24 total.

7. To make the strip sets, stitch each light green strip to a yellow dot strip along the long edges. Make six. The strip sets should measure 2½" wide when sewn. Crosscut the strip sets into 48 segments, 4½" wide.

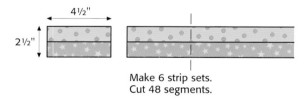

Make 6 strip sets.
Cut 48 segments.

8. Join a pink-and-orange stripe rectangle to 14 of the segments from step 7 as shown.

Make 14.

ASSEMBLING THE QUILT TOP

1. Arrange the embellished blocks, the large and small appliquéd blocks, the half-square-triangle units, the yellow-and-green strip-set segments, and the yellow-green-and-pink units into nine rows as shown. Sew the pieces in each row together as shown, and then join the rows to complete the center quilt design.

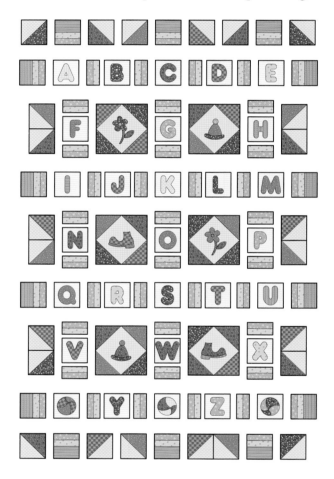

2. Refer to "Adding Borders" on page 71 to cut the remaining five 1½" x 42" yellow dot print strips to the correct lengths for the inner border; stitch them to the quilt top. Repeat with the 3½" x 42" blue print strips for the outer border.

FINISHING

REFER TO "Quilt Finishing" on pages 71–75.

1. Layer the quilt top with batting and backing; baste.

2. Quilt as desired. The center quilt design of the featured project was machine quilted with simple arcs, diagonal Xs, and along the seam lines. Graduating loops decorate the outside triangles, and stippling enhances the blue border.

3. Trim the backing and batting even with the quilt top.

4. Bind the quilt with the 2½" x 42" blue print strips.

5. Add a label.

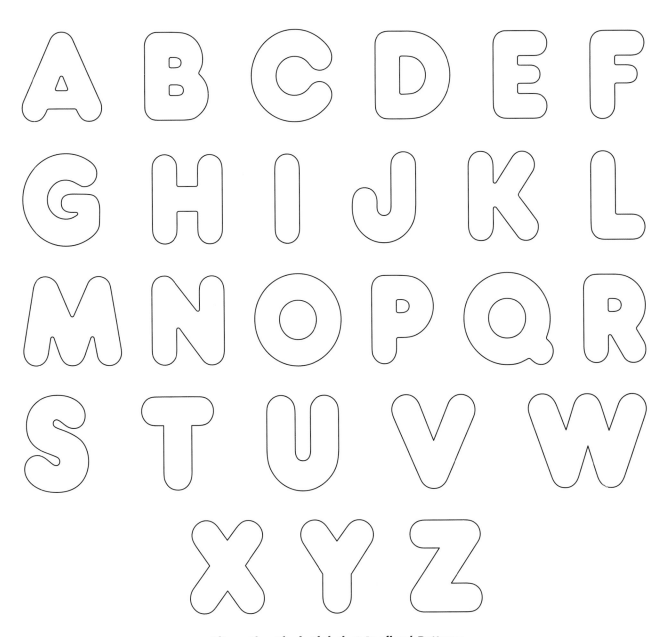

Alternative Block Alphabet Appliqué Patterns
Enlarge 300%.

Large Appliqué Block Patterns

6

5

7

1

2

3

4

10

11

8

9

12
Cut ball as one piece.

14

13

**Small Appliqué
Block Patterns**

LOVELY LITTLE CRAZY QUILT

By Jennifer Lokey, 35" x 35". Quilted by Betty Braud.

Crazy quilts have always been a showcase for embroidery. For the machine embroiderer, this is a perfect opportunity to use small digitized designs. The addition of small border laces and decorative machine stitches create a refreshingly quick and lovely little Crazy quilt for those of us who love the look but just don't have the time. For those whose love and skill are hand embroidery, construct this quilt as instructed, adding creative hand stitching at the point that the machine-embroidery motifs would be applied.

MATERIALS

Yardage is based on 42"-wide fabric.

- 1 yard of black fabric for blocks, sashing rectangles, and binding
- ½ yard *each* of the following fabrics for blocks, sashing squares, and border: light gold, medium gold, dark gold, light red, medium red, dark red, green, off-white with black print, and black with off-white print
- 1⅛ yards of fabric for backing
- 40" x 40" square of batting
- 3½ yards of 22"-wide lightweight interfacing for foundations
- Digitized embroidery designs of your choice that stitch out to approximately 1¼" x 1¼". The collection of small digitized designs used in this wall quilt is by Cactus Punch, Design Pack LIL02.
- Tear-away stabilizer
- Temporary spray adhesive
- Sulky 40-weight rayon embroidery threads: Black (1005), Mine Gold (1025), Medium Tawny Tan (1056), Off White (1071), Pastel Yellow (1135), Yellow Orange (1137), True Orange (1168), Bayberry Red (1169), Medium Dark Avocado (1176), Avocado (1177), Dusty Navy (1198), Medium Maple (1216), Dark Periwinkle (1226), Salmon Peach (1259)
- 2 yards *each* of 4 different ⅜"- to ⅝"-wide flat laces

CUTTING

NOTE: *The fabric left over after cutting the following pieces will be used to foundation piece the blocks and border units.*

From the interfacing, cut:
- 9 squares, 9" x 9"
- 24 rectangles, 2½" x 7½"
- 16 squares, 2½" x 2½"
- 18 rectangles, 4½" x 10"

From the black, cut:
- 10 strips, 2½" x 42"; crosscut 6 strips into 24 rectangles, 2½" x 7½"

From the sashing square fabrics, cut a *total* of:
- 16 squares, 2½" x 2½"

MAKING THE BLOCKS AND BORDER UNITS

1. To make the block foundations, use a pencil or permanent marker to trace the block pattern on page 39 onto each of the 9" x 9" interfacing squares. To make the border unit foundations, trace the border unit pattern on page 38 onto each of the 4½" x 10" interfacing rectangles. The patterns include a ¼" seam allowance. Be sure to copy the circled numbers onto the foundations; you will follow these for the piecing sequence. The measurements listed under each circled number indicate the size to cut the fabric piece for that area; they do not need to be transferred to the pattern.

2. To foundation piece each block and border unit, randomly select a piece of fabric from the leftover block and border fabrics and cut it to the measurement indicated on the original pattern for the shape labeled 1. Pin this piece, right side up, over the shape labeled 1 on the *unmarked* side of the foundation. Be sure the fabric piece overlaps the shape on all sides by at least ¼". Cut the fabric for shape 2 to the size indicated and place it right sides together over the fabric for shape 1, with one edge approximately ¼" over the line between shapes 1 and 2 as shown. Check to be sure that shape 1 is covered by the fabric piece. You can do this by carefully lifting up the fabric edges or holding the pieces up to a light source. Now check to be sure that the fabric piece for shape 2 will cover the shape when it is stitched in place and pressed open. Make any adjustments necessary. Place pins perpendicular to the seam line between shapes 1 and 2 when you are satisfied with the fabric placement.

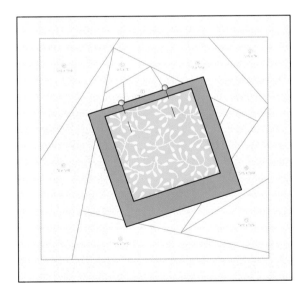

NOTE: *You can cut all the pieces for each block and border unit before beginning the piecing process if desired, but be sure to randomly select fabrics for each piece to maintain the look of the traditional crazy quilt design and ensure that each block is different.*

3. With the *marked* side of the foundation up, stitch along the seam line between shapes 1 and 2.

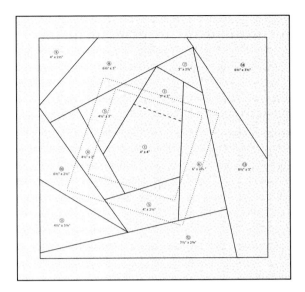

4. Fold the foundation away from the fabric pieces and trim the seam to ¼", using a rotary cutter and ruler.

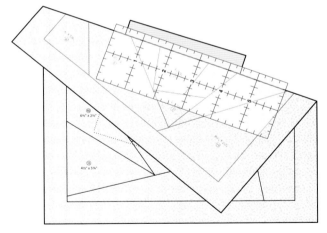

Trim seam to ¼".

5. From the fabric side, finger-press the fabric piece for shape 2 away from the fabric piece for shape 1 so that it covers shape 2.

6. Cut a fabric piece for shape 3. Align, pin, sew, and trim the piece in the same manner as the fabric piece for shape 2.

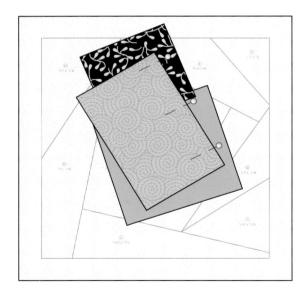

7. Continue cutting fabric pieces and applying them to the foundation in this manner, working in numerical order, until all of the shapes are covered. When you complete all of the blocks and border units, trim each foundation along the outer marked line.

8. To make the side borders, stitch four border units together end to end, rotating the blocks as desired to create a randomly pieced look. Make two. Stitch five border units together end to end in the same manner to make the top and bottom borders. Make two.

   NOTE: *The borders are longer than necessary. They will be cut to the exact lengths before they are added to the quilt top.*

Side Borders
Make 2.

Top and Bottom Borders
Make 2.

9. Choose and mark the direction of each border—left side, right side, top, and bottom. This will help determine the direction of the machine embroidery if you intend to designate a top and bottom for your quilt.

10. To embellish the blocks and borders with machine embroidery, hoop the stabilizer first. Spray the back of a block or a section of a border with temporary fabric adhesive. Center the area to be embroidered on the hooped stabilizer. Run the machine through the step of showing the boundaries of the sewing area, if your machine has this capability. Reposition the block or border placement on the stabilizer, if necessary, to sew within the chosen area on the block or border. Be sure to plan the motif placement so that it falls within the seam allowances. Do not place any motifs near the ends of the border units; they may be trimmed away when the border strips are cut to the exact measurements to fit the quilt top.

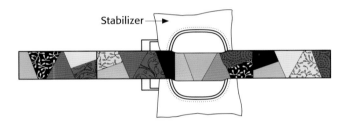

Stabilizer

11. Refer to "Machine-Embroidery Basics" on page 9 to sew out as many designs as you like on the blocks and borders.

12. Embellish selected seam lines on the blocks and borders with decorative machine stitching and/or flat lace. You do not need to embellish every seam line. For decorative stitching, use the same thread colors used for the machine embroidery. To embellish with lace, cut a piece of lace the length of the seam line to be covered and straight stitch it in place with matching thread. Backstitch at the beginning and end.

ASSEMBLING THE QUILT TOP

1. Pin a matching interfacing piece to the wrong side of each sashing rectangle and sashing square. This is to keep a consistent fabric weight throughout the quilt top.

2. Arrange the blocks, sashing rectangles, and sashing squares into rows as shown. Stitch the pieces in each row together, keeping the interfacing pieces aligned with their matching fabric piece. Press the seams toward the sashing rectangles. Stitch the rows together to complete the center quilt design.

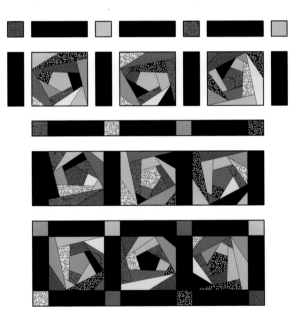

3. Refer to "Adding Borders" on page 71 to cut the embellished side border strips to the length measured and stitch them to the quilt top. Repeat with the embellished top and bottom border strips.

FINISHING

REFER TO "Quilt Finishing" on pages 71–75.

1. Layer the quilt top with batting and backing; baste.

2. Quilt as desired. The featured quilt was machine quilted along each seam line.

3. Trim the backing and batting even with the quilt top.

4. Bind the quilt with the remaining 2½" x 42" black strips.

5. Add a label.

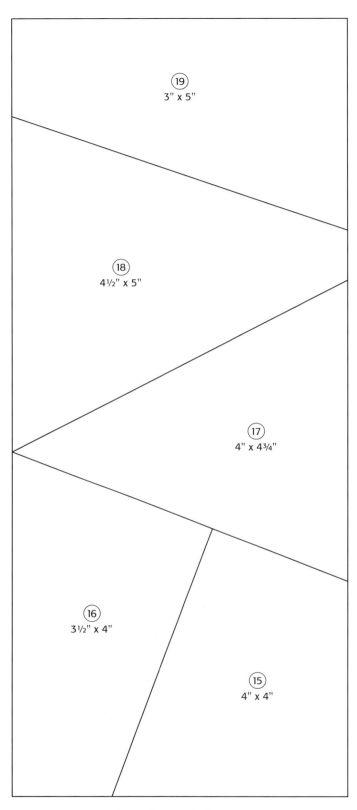

Border Unit Foundation Pattern

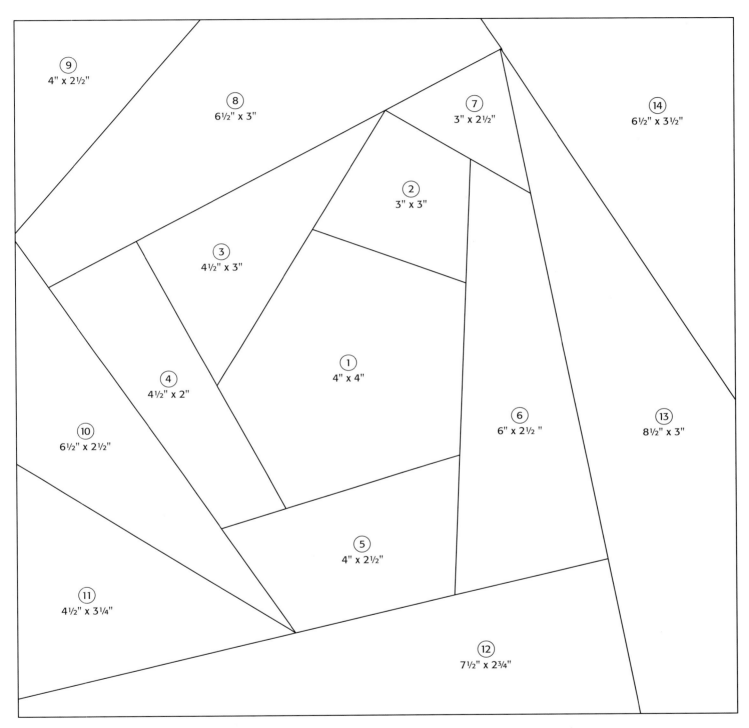

Block Foundation Pattern

FLOWERS IN A BASKET

By Jennifer Lokey, 44½" x 60". Quilted by Allison Bayer.

This charming little bouquet of embroidered flowers enhances the delicate pieced basket to create a delightful, airy quilt design. The challenge was to add variety, thus the different basket colors and embroidery thread colors. The threads were chosen with the fabrics in hand so that the color effect would be pleasing.

MATERIALS

Yardage is based on 42"-wide fabric.

For the machine-embroidered project:
♦ 2⅜ yards of light yellow print for embellished blocks
♦ 1¾ yards of blue print for sashing strips and binding
♦ ¾ yard of medium yellow print for sashing strips and sashing squares
♦ ¼ yard *each* of the following fabrics for baskets: 3 different blue prints, 2 different red prints, 2 different green prints, 2 different lavender prints, and 1 pink print
♦ 3 yards of fabric for backing
♦ 50" x 65" piece of batting
♦ Digitized embroidery design of your choice that stitches out to approximately 2¾" x 3¾". The floral wreath design used in the featured project is by Oklahoma Embroidery Supply and Design, Floral Pack #10212, design FL069.
♦ Tear-away stabilizer
♦ Isacord 40-weight polyester embroidery threads: Toffee (842), Old Gold (851), Strawberry Red (1805), Corsage Pink (1840), Wild Iris (2830), Lavender (3040), Reef Blue (3815), Oxford Blue (3840), Swiss Ivy Green (5422)
♦ Freezer paper or fusible web, depending on the appliqué method used

APPLIQUÉ ALTERNATIVE

You can easily substitute a cluster of fabric yo-yos and appliquéd leaves for the embroidered motif if you prefer.

For the alternative yo-yo and appliqué design:
You will need the same amount of blue print for sashing and binding, medium yellow for sashing squares, backing, and batting as the embroidered project, as well as the following:
♦ 1⅞ yards of light yellow print for block backgrounds
♦ ⅜ yard of each basket fabric listed
♦ Freezer paper or fusible web, depending on the appliqué method used
♦ Quilting thread
♦ Hand-sewing needle
♦ Threads for finishing appliqué edges (optional)

CUTTING

All measurements include ¼"-wide seam allowances.

From the light yellow print, cut:

♦ 4 strips, 9" x 42"; crosscut the strips into 20 rectangles, 8" x 9"*

♦ 4 strips, 3" x 42"; crosscut the strips into 40 squares, 3" x 3"

♦ 18 strips, 1½" x 42"; crosscut the strips into:
  40 strips, 1½" x 7½"
  40 strips, 1½" x 8½"

If you will be embellishing the blocks with yo-yos, cut 4 strips, 5" x 42"; crosscut the strips into 20 rectangles, 5" x 6½".

From *each* of the 2 red prints, 1 pink print, 1 lavender print, 2 blue prints, and 2 green prints for baskets, cut:

♦ 2 rectangles (16 total), 3" x 6½"

♦ 4 squares (32 total), 2" x 2"

From the remaining lavender print, cut:

♦ 3 rectangles, 3" x 6½"

♦ 6 squares, 2" x 2"

From the remaining blue print for baskets, cut:

♦ 1 rectangle, 3" x 6½"

♦ 2 squares, 2" x 2"

From the blue print for sashing and binding, cut:

♦ 26 strips, 1½" x 42"

♦ 6 strips, 2½" x 42"

From the medium yellow print, cut:

♦ 13 strips, 1" x 42"

♦ 3 strips, 3" x 42"; crosscut the strips into 30 squares, 3" x 3"

MAKING THE BLOCKS

FOR THE machine-embroidered project, follow these steps:

1. Refer to "Machine-Embroidery Basics" on page 9 to stitch the selected design on each 8" x 9" light yellow rectangle. Use several combinations of different thread colors to embroider each rectangle to create variety in the finished quilt.

2. Refer to "Trimming the Embellished Pieces" on page 15 to measure and mark the horizontal center of each embroidered design. Measure 3¼" to the left and right of the center point and mark the side trim lines. Measure ½" down from the lower edge of the stitched design and mark the lower trim line. Measure 5" up from the lower trim line and mark the upper trim line. Cut on the drawn lines to create a 5" x 6½" embellished rectangle.

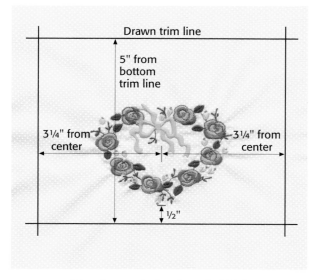

Mark horizontal center.

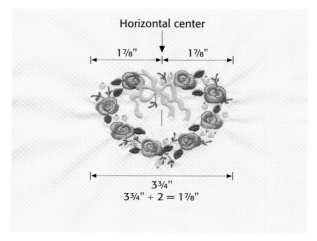

Trim piece to 6½" wide and 5" high.

3. To make the basket base, draw a diagonal line on the wrong side of each of the 2" x 2" squares for baskets. Place a square on one corner of each 3" light yellow square, right sides together. Sew on the marked line; trim ¼" from the stitched line and press the seam toward the triangle corner. Make 40 total.

4. Draw a diagonal line on the wrong side of each unit from step 3 as shown. Select two matching units and place them as shown, right sides together, on a 3" x 6½" rectangle that matches the triangle color of each unit. Sew on the marked lines; trim ¼" from the stitching lines and press the seam toward the large triangle. Repeat with the remaining units and 3" x 6½" rectangles. Make 20 total.

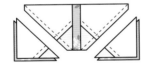

5. Sew an embroidered 5" x 6½" rectangle to each basket base as shown.

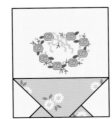

6. Join a 1½" x 7½" light yellow strip to the sides of each basket unit. Join a 1½" x 8½" light yellow strip to the top and bottom of each basket unit.

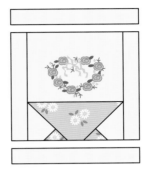

7. Refer to "Appliqué Basics" on page 11 to make a matching handle for each Basket block, using the remaining basket fabrics and the pattern on page 45. Appliqué the handles in place, aligning the handle ends with the ends of the basket base upper edge. Make 20 Basket blocks. The blocks should measure 8½" x 9½".

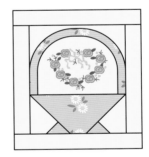

Make 20 total.

For the alternative appliquéd design, follow these steps:

1. Refer to "Appliqué Basics" on page 11 to prepare and cut 40 leaf appliqués from the remaining green fabrics, using the pattern on page 45. Refer to "Yo-Yo Embellishment" on page 12 to make 100 medium yo-yos and 40 large yo-yos from the remaining red, pink, lavender, and blue basket fabrics, using the patterns on page 45. Set the leaf appliqués and yo-yos aside; they will be applied to the blocks later.

2. Refer to steps 3–7 of the machine-embroidered block instructions to make the blocks, substituting the 5" x 6½" light yellow rectangle for the embroidered rectangle in step 5.

3. Temporarily arrange two leaves, five small yo-yos, and two large yo-yos between the basket base and handle of each block as desired, referring to the photo on page 41 for placement help. Remove the yo-yos and appliqué the leaves in place. Reposition the yo-yos and tack them in several places to secure them to the block.

   NOTE: *This step may be done after the quilt is completed, if desired.*

ASSEMBLING THE QUILT TOP

1. To make the sashing strip sets, stitch a 1½" x 42" blue print strip to both long edges of each 1" x 42" medium yellow strip as shown. Make 13. The strip sets should measure 3" wide when sewn. Crosscut the strip sets into 24 seg-ments, 8½" long, and 25 seg-ments, 9½" long.

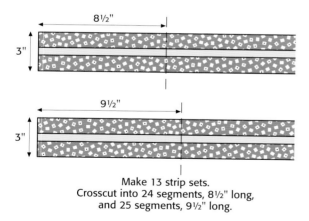

Make 13 strip sets.
Crosscut into 24 segments, 8½" long,
and 25 segments, 9½" long.

2. Arrange the Basket blocks, the sashing segments, and the 3" medium yellow squares into rows as shown. Sew the pieces in each row together. Press the seams toward the sashing

segments. Join the rows to complete the quilt top. Press the seams toward the sashing rows.

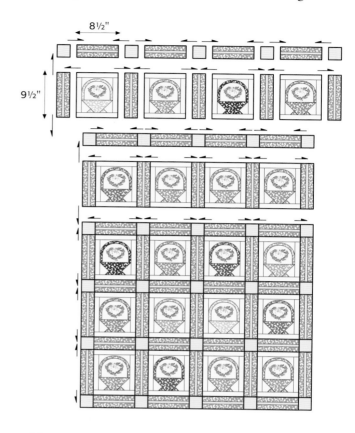

FINISHING

REFER TO "Quilt Finishing" on pages 71–75.

1. Layer the quilt top with batting and backing; baste.

2. Quilt as desired. The backgrounds of the blocks in the featured quilt were stipple stitched. The sashing segments were quilted along the seam lines, with the lines continuing into the sashing squares.

3. Trim the backing and batting even with the quilt top.

4. Bind the quilt with the 2½" x 42" blue print strips.

5. Add a label.

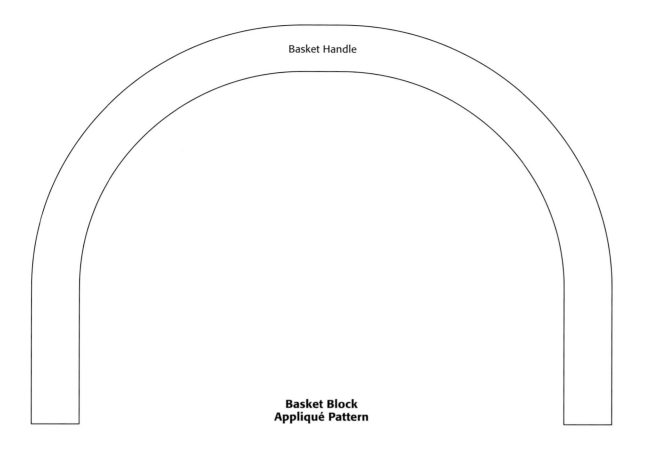

Basket Handle

**Basket Block
Appliqué Pattern**

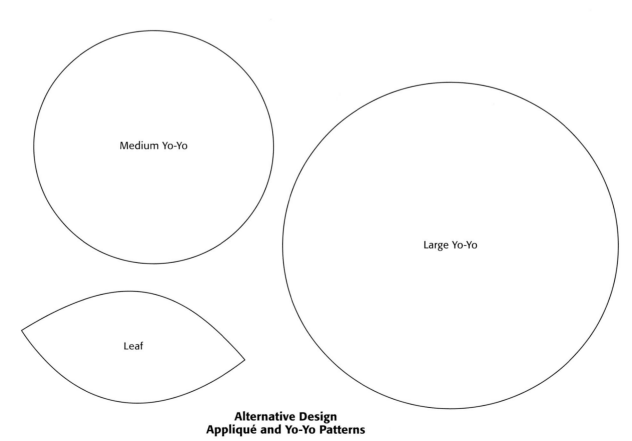

Medium Yo-Yo

Large Yo-Yo

Leaf

**Alternative Design
Appliqué and Yo-Yo Patterns**

GARDEN STEPPING-STONES

By Jennifer Lokey, 68⅛" x 68⅛". Quilted by Allison Bayer.

The ever-popular hand-embroidered redwork has been beautifully interpreted in digitized machine embroidery for those who love the look. I chose these delicate flower designs from Cactus Punch and added some traditional piecing to highlight the embroidery. The title "Garden Stepping-Stones" seemed to fit perfectly with the addition of the single half-square-triangle unit in the alternate block. If you prefer to travel the more traditional hand-embroidery route, a plethora of redwork patterns are available for that purpose.

MATERIALS

Yardage is based on 42"-wide fabric.

For the machine-embroidered project:
- 2½ yards of white solid for block backgrounds and inner border
- 1½ yards of bright red print #1 for outer border and binding
- 1⅛ yards of bright red print #2 for setting triangles
- ⅝ yard *each* of 2 different light red prints for sashing
- ⅝ yard *each* of 2 different medium red prints for sashing
- ⅝ yard *each* of 4 different bright red prints #3–#6 for sashing (two of these prints can be the same red prints used for the setting triangles and outer border, if desired)
- 8 yards of medium-size red rickrack
- 4¼ yards of fabric for backing
- 73" x 73" square of batting
- Tear-away stabilizer
- Heat-erasable marking pen
- Temporary spray adhesive
- Digitized embroidery design of your choice that stitches out to approximately 3½" x 3½". The group of designs used in the featured quilt are by Cactus Punch, Quilting Volume 5, Redwork 2.
- 1 large spool (850 yards) of Sulky Bayberry Red (1169) 40-weight embroidery thread

For the alternative hand-embroidered design:
You will need the fabrics and batting listed for the machine-embroidered project, as well as the following:
- Hand-embroidery redwork designs of your choice that measure approximately 3½" x 3½"
- DMC Red Fruit (816) #8 pearl cotton
- Hand-embroidery needle

CUTTING

All measurements include ¼"-wide seam allowances.

From the white solid, cut:
- 5 strips, 8" x 42"; crosscut the strips into 25 squares, 8" x 8"
- 15 strips, 2½" x 42"; crosscut 8 strips into:
    32 squares, 2½" x 2½"
    32 rectangles, 2½" x 6½"

From the tear-away stabilizer, cut:
- 25 squares, 8" x 8"

From *each* of the 2 different light red prints, cut:
- 1 rectangle (2 total), 17" x 30"

From *each* of the 2 different medium red prints, cut:
- 1 rectangle (2 total), 17" x 30"
- 10 squares (20 total), 2½" x 2½"

From *each* of bright red prints #3–#6, cut:
♦ 1 rectangle (4 total), 17" x 30"
♦ 10 squares (40 total), 2½" x 2½"

From bright red print #2, cut:
♦ 4 squares, 12⅝" x 12⅝"; cut each square in half twice diagonally to yield 16 side setting triangles
♦ 2 squares, 8" x 8"; cut each square in half once diagonally to yield 4 corner setting triangles

From bright red print #1, cut:
♦ 8 strips, 3" x 42"
♦ 8 strips, 2½" x 42"

MAKING THE EMBELLISHED BLOCKS

FOR THE machine-embroidered project, follow these steps:

1. Fold each 8" x 8" white square in half diagonally in both directions. Using the heat-erasable marking pen, mark the diagonal center of each square with an X.

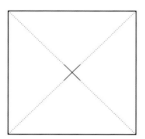

2. Referring to "Machine-Embroidery Basics" on page 9, hoop a square of stabilizer. Mark the center of the stabilizer lightly with a pencil, using the marks on the embroidery hoop to assist in determining the center point.

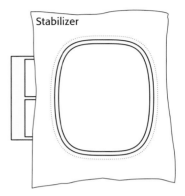

3. Spray the wrong side of a fabric square from step 1 with temporary spray adhesive and position it onto the stabilizer on point, matching the center marks. Insert the hoop into the machine and stitch out the desired design.

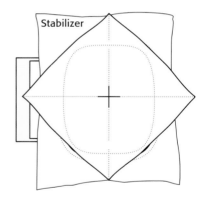

4. Repeat steps 2 and 3 with the remaining 8" x 8" fabric and stabilizer squares. When all of the squares have been stitched, remove the stabilizer and follow the manufacturer's instructions to remove the center marks on the fabric squares.

5. Because the designs have been sewn on point and the trimming lines will be determined on the straight grain, measure on the diagonal of the design to determine the center of each design, using the method described in "Trimming the Embellished Pieces" on page 15. Once the center has been determined, measure 3¼" from the center in each direction and mark the lines for trimming. Cut each square on the drawn lines to create a 6½" x 6½" embellished block.

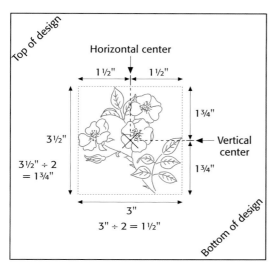

Determine design center.

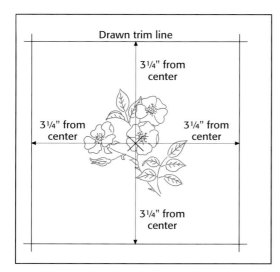

Trim piece to 6½" x 6½".

For the alternative hand-embroidered design, follow these steps:

1. Fold each 8" x 8" white square in half diagonally in both directions. Finger-press the fold lines to mark the center of each square.

2. Refer to "Hand-Embroidery Basics" on page 14 to transfer the desired design to the center of each 8" x 8" white square. Refer to the pattern instructions to embroider the designs, using the pearl cotton.

3. Refer to step 5 of the machine-embroidered block instructions to trim the squares to 6½" x 6½".

MAKING THE ALTERNATE BLOCKS AND SASHING UNITS

1. To make the half-square-triangle units for the alternate block centers and the sashing units, use a pencil or water-soluble marker to draw a grid of five rows of eight 2⅞" squares *each* on the wrong side of the two 17" x 30" light red print and medium red print rectangles, leaving no space between the squares and rows as shown. Draw a diagonal line through each square. Place each marked rectangle right sides together with a 17" x 30" bright red print #3–#6 rectangle. Pin the layers together between the diagonal lines. Sew ¼" from both sides of each diagonal line.

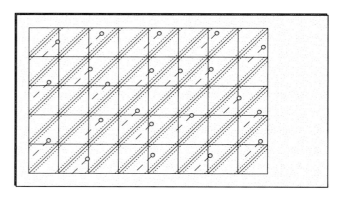

2. Cut along each diagonal, vertical, and horizontal line. This will yield 80 half-square-triangle units from each of the combinations (320 total). You will use 316 and have 4 left over. Open each unit and press the seam toward the bright red triangle. Cut away the extended corners.

Make 320 total.

3. To make the alternate blocks, stitch a 2½" x 2½" white square to each side of 16 medium-and-bright-red half-square-triangle units, positioning the unit seam as shown. Press the seams toward the white squares.

Make 16.

4. Stitch a 2½" x 6½" white rectangle to the top and bottom of each unit from step 3 to complete the blocks. Press the seams toward the white rectangles. Make 16 alternate blocks.

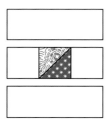 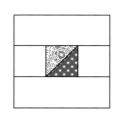

Make 16.

5. Stitch three of the remaining half-square-triangle units together as shown to make a sashing unit. Make 100.

Make 100.

ASSEMBLING THE QUILT TOP

1. Arrange the embellished blocks, the alternate blocks, the sashing units, and the 2½" red print squares into 19 diagonal rows as shown. Sew the pieces in each row together, and then sew the rows into groups as shown. Add a side setting triangle to the ends of the grouped rows as shown. Stitch all of the rows together and then add the corner setting triangles.

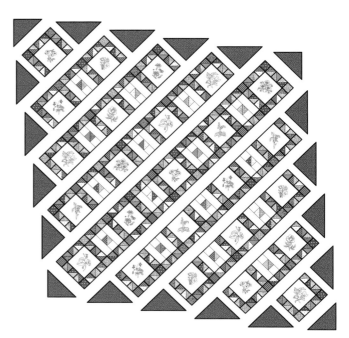

Quilt Assembly Diagram

2. Measure ¼" from the point of the 2½" squares and trim the quilt edges.

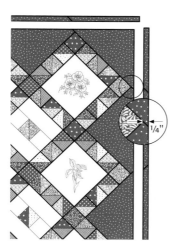

3. Refer to "Adding Borders" on page 71 to cut the seven remaining 2½" x 42" white strips to the correct lengths and stitch them to the quilt top. Repeat with the 3" x 42" bright red #1 strips.

FINISHING

Refer to "Quilt Finishing" on pages 71–75.

1. Layer the quilt top with batting and backing; baste.

2. Quilt as desired. The featured project was machine quilted along the seam lines of the half-square-triangle units. The embroidered blocks feature a cameo circle around each of the redwork designs with a line of quilting crossing the block points. The quilting within the alternate blocks gives a crosshatch effect. A graduating loop fills in the side and corner setting triangles, with a more open loop in the outer border. A quilting line was stitched down the center of the white border to hold the border as well as give a guideline for adding the rickrack when the quilting was finished.

3. Center the rickrack on the inner border and stitch it in place with matching thread.

4. Trim the backing and batting even with the quilt top.

5. Bind the quilt with the 2½" x 42" bright red print #2 strips.

6. Add a label.

FLOWER BURSTS

By Jennifer Lokey, 27" x 27". Quilted by Monica Rodarmer.

The joyful expression of this single embroidered flower blossom beckoned me to incorporate it into a quilt block. The creative process was such fun. As you can see, the geometric shapes come alive with purpose as they frame this freedom-loving little flower, and the vibrant colors add excitement.

MATERIALS

Yardage is based on 42"-wide fabric.

For the machine-embroidered project:
- 1 yard of green fabric for blocks
- ¾ yard of coral fabric for blocks and binding
- ½ yard of purple fabric for blocks
- ⅜ yard of yellow fabric for blocks and border
- 1 yard of fabric for backing
- 31" x 31" square of batting
- Digitized embroidery design of your choice that stitches out to approximately 3" x 3". The flower blossom design used in the featured project is by Zundt Design, Number 200267.
- Tear-away stabilizer
- 1 large spool (850 yards) of Sulky Yellow (1023) 40-weight rayon embroidery thread
- 1 small spool (250 yards) of Sulky Red Geranium (1188) 40-weight rayon embroidery thread

For the alternative appliquéd design:
You will need the fabrics and batting listed for the embroidered project, as well as the following:
- ⅛ yard extra of yellow and coral for appliqués
- Threads for finishing appliqué edges (optional)

APPLIQUÉ ALTERNATIVE

An equally radiant appliquéd flower can be used in place of the embroidered design if you choose.

CUTTING

All measurements include ¼"-wide seam allowances.

From the purple fabric, cut:
- 1 strip, 9" x 42"; crosscut the strip into 5 rectangles, 8" x 9"
- 1 strip, 2" x 10"

From the coral fabric, cut:
- 1 rectangle, 10" x 20"
- 2 strips, 1¾" x 42"; crosscut the strips into 4 strips, 1¾" x 16"
- 3 strips, 2½" x 42"

From the green fabric, cut:
- ♦ 1 rectangle, 10" x 20"
- ♦ 2 strips, 5⅛" x 42"; crosscut the strips into 10 squares, 5⅛" x 5⅛". Cut each square in half once diagonally to yield 20 triangles.
- ♦ 1 strip, 1½" x 42"; crosscut the strip into 8 rectangles, 1½" x 4½"
- ♦ 2 strips, 1¾" x 42"; crosscut the strips into 8 rectangles, 1¾" x 6½"
- ♦ 1 strip, 2" x 16"
- ♦ 2 strips, 1¾" x 10"
- ♦ 1 strip, 4½" x 14"
- ♦ 1 strip, 6½" x 16"

From the yellow fabric, cut:
- ♦ 2 strips, 1½" x 42"; crosscut the strips into:
   20 squares, 1½" x 1½"
   2 strips, 1½" x 14"
- ♦ 4 strips, 1¼" x 42"

MAKING THE BLOCKS

1. To make the embellished blocks, machine embroider or appliqué the 8" x 9" purple rectangles. If you choose to machine embroider, refer to "Machine-Embroidery Basics" on page 9.

   If you choose to appliqué, refer to "Appliqué Basics" on page 11 to prepare and cut the appliqués from the appropriate fabrics, using the patterns on page 57. Trace and cut out five of appliqué 1 from the yellow fabric and five of appliqué 2 from the coral fabric.

2. Refer to "Trimming the Embellished Pieces" on page 15 to trim each embellished rectangle to 4½" x 4½".

3. To make the half-square-triangle units for the embellished blocks, use a pencil or water-soluble marker to draw a grid of four rows of ten 1⅞" squares *each* on the wrong side of the 10" x 20" coral rectangle, leaving no space between the squares and rows as shown. Draw a diagonal line through each square. Place the marked rectangle right sides together with the 10" x 20" green rectangle. Pin the layers together between the diagonal lines. Sew ¼" from both sides of each diagonal line.

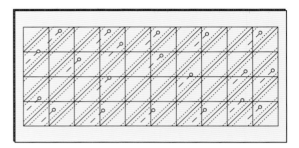

4. Cut along each diagonal, vertical, and horizontal line. This will yield 80 half-square-triangle units. Open each unit and press the seam toward the green fabric. Cut away the extended corners.

Make 80.

5. Stitch four half-square-triangle units into a row as shown. Make 20. Press the seams in one direction.

Make 20.

6. Arrange four rows from step 5, four 1½" x 1½" yellow squares, and one embellished square into three horizontal rows as shown. Stitch the pieces in each row together, and then sew the rows together. Make five units.

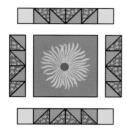 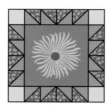

Make 5.

7. To complete the embellished blocks, sew a green triangle to each side of each unit from step 6, stitching opposite sides first. Press the seams toward the green triangles. The blocks should measure 9" x 9".

Make 5.

8. To make the alternate blocks, make one strip set *each* of strip sets A–D as shown. Press the seam allowances toward the green strips. Cross-cut each strip set into the appropriate width segments.

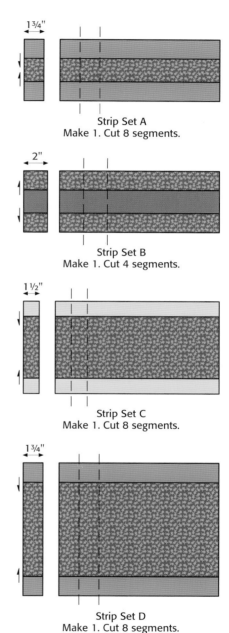

1¾"

Strip Set A
Make 1. Cut 8 segments.

2"

Strip Set B
Make 1. Cut 4 segments.

1½"

Strip Set C
Make 1. Cut 8 segments.

1¾"

Strip Set D
Make 1. Cut 8 segments.

9. Sew two segments from strip set A and one segment from strip set B together as shown. Make four units.

Make 4.

10. Stitch a 1½" x 4½" green rectangle to the sides of each unit from step 9, and then stitch a segment from strip set C to the top and bottom of each unit. Press the seams toward the newly added pieces.

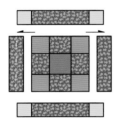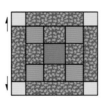

11. To complete the alternate blocks, stitch a 1¾" x 6½" green rectangle to the sides of each unit from step 10. Then sew a segment from strip set D to the top and bottom of each unit. Press the seams toward the newly added pieces. The blocks should measure 9" x 9".

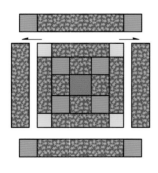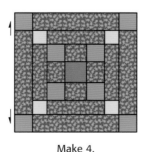

Make 4.

ASSEMBLING THE QUILT TOP

1. Refer to the quilt assembly diagram to arrange the embellished blocks and alternate blocks into three rows of three blocks each, alternating the blocks in each row as shown. Stitch the blocks in each row together, and then stitch the rows together to complete the center design area.

2. Refer to "Adding Borders" on page 71 to cut the 1¼" x 42" yellow strips to the correct lengths and stitch them to the quilt top.

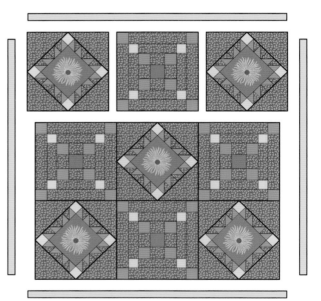

Quilt Assembly Diagram

FINISHING

REFER TO "Quilt Finishing" on pages 71–75.

1. Layer the quilt top with batting and backing; baste.

2. Quilt as desired. The featured quilt was quilted along each seam line. The outer triangles of the embellished blocks were stipple stiched, and a single line of quilting was stitched ¼" within the seam line of the purple squares to highlight the embellished design.

3. Trim the backing and batting even with the quilt top.

4. Bind the quilt with the 2½" x 42" coral strips.

5. Add a label.

**Alternative Block
Appliqué Patterns**

TEA AT MY HOUSE

By Jennifer Lokey, 47" x 57". Quilted by Allison Bayer.

W hen I came across these whimsical little teapot house motifs from Amazing Designs, I just had to share them with you in a friendly, familiar quilt block design. Don't you think a cozy log cabin would be a perfect place to have a cup of tea?

MATERIALS

Yardage is based on 42"-wide fabric.

For the machine-embroidered project:

♦ 1⅛ yards of light yellow solid for embellished blocks

♦ 1⅛ yards of light green print for block logs, inner border, and binding

♦ 1 yard of coral print for block logs and outer border

♦ ½ yard of medium green print for block logs

♦ ½ yard of blue-green print for block logs

♦ ½ yard of yellow print for block logs

♦ ½ yard of pink print for block logs

♦ ⅜ yard of medium blue tone-on-tone print for block logs

♦ ⅜ yard of pink tone-on-tone print for block logs

♦ 3⅛ yards of fabric for backing

♦ 51" x 61" piece of batting

♦ Digitized embroidery design of your choice that stitches out to approximately 3¾" x 3¾". The teapot house designs in the featured quilt are by Amazing Designs, Tea Pot Birdhouses, AD1289.

♦ Tear-away stabilizer

♦ Sulky 40-weight rayon embroidery threads: Autumn Gold (523), Lipstick Red (561), Moss Green (630), Soft White (1002), Dark Peach (1020), Yellow (1023), Medium Blue (1029), Medium Orchid (1031), True Red (1039), Grass Green (1049), Pale Peach

APPLIQUÉ ALTERNATIVE

If desired, choose the alternative heart appliqué to bring another kind of warmth to this charming quilt.

(1064), Lemon Yellow (1067), Tangerine (1078), Ecru (1082), Silver (1085), Dark Ecru (1128), Brown (1129), Yellow Orange (1137), Temple Gold (1159), Avocado (1177), Dark Purple (1195), Blue (1196), Medium Maple (1216), Chestnut (1217), Gray (1219), Light Baby Blue (1222), Bright Pink (1224), Classic Green (1232), Smokey Gray (1240), Orange Flame (1246), Bright Peacock Blue (1252), Toast (1266), Dark Nickel Gray (1329), Lime Green (1510), Light Rose (1533), Team Blue (1535)

For the alternative appliquéd design:
You will need the fabrics and batting listed for the embroidered project, as well as the following:
- ⅛ yard extra of each block log fabric for appliqués
- Freezer paper or fusible web, depending on the appliqué method used
- Threads for finishing appliqué edges (optional)

CUTTING

All measurements include ¼"-wide seam allowances.

From the light yellow solid, cut:
- 4 strips, 9" x 42"; crosscut the strips into 20 rectangles, 8" x 9"

From the light green print, cut:
- 7 strips, 1¼" x 42"; crosscut the strips into:
    10 rectangles, 1¼" x 5"
    10 rectangles, 1¼" x 5¾"
    10 rectangles, 1¼" x 7¼"
    10 rectangles, 1¼" x 8"
- 5 strips, 1½" x 42"
- 6 strips, 2½" x 42"

From the medium green print, cut:
- 11 strips, 1¼" x 42"; crosscut the strips into:
    10 strips, 1¼" x 8"
    10 strips, 1¼" x 8¾"
    10 strips, 1¼" x 10¼"
    10 strips, 1¼" x 11"

From the blue-green print, cut:
- 11 strips, 1¼" x 42"; crosscut the strips into:
    10 strips, 1¼" x 8¾"
    20 strips, 1¼" x 9½"
    10 strips, 1¼" x 10¼"

From the medium blue tone-on-tone print, cut:
- 7 strips, 1¼" x 42"; crosscut the strips into:
    10 strips, 1¼" x 5¾"
    20 strips, 1¼" x 6½"
    10 strips, 1¼" x 7¼"

From the yellow print, cut:
- 11 strips, 1¼" x 42"; crosscut the strips into:
    10 strips, 1¼" x 8¾"
    20 strips, 1¼" x 9½"
    10 strips, 1¼" x 10¼"

From the pink tone-on-tone print, cut:
- 7 strips, 1¼" x 42"; crosscut the strips into:
    10 strips, 1¼" x 5¾"
    20 strips, 1¼" x 6½"
    10 strips, 1¼" x 7¼"

From the pink print, cut:
- 11 strips, 1¼" x 42"; crosscut the strips into:
    10 strips, 1¼" x 8"
    10 strips, 1¼" x 8¾"
    10 strips, 1¼" x 10¼"
    10 strips, 1¼" x 11"

From the coral print, cut:
- 7 strips, 1¼" x 42"; crosscut the strips into:
    10 strips, 1¼" x 5"
    10 strips, 1¼" x 5¾"
    10 strips, 1¼" x 7¼"
    10 strips, 1¼" x 8"
- 6 strips, 3" x 42"

MAKING THE BLOCKS

1. To make the embellished blocks, machine embroider or appliqué each 8" x 9" light yellow rectangle with the chosen design. If you choose to machine embroider, refer to "Machine-Embroidery Basics" on page 9.

    If you choose to appliqué, refer to "Appliqué Basics" on page 11 to prepare and cut 20 heart appliqués from the remaining block log fabrics, using the pattern on page 62.

2. Refer to "Trimming the Embellished Pieces" on page 15 to trim each embellished rectangle to 5" x 5".

3. Lay out one embellished square and the log strips for block A as shown. Begin by stitching the 1¼" x 5" light green log to the right-hand side of the embellished square. Working counterclockwise, continue adding the logs to the square in the order shown. Press the seams away from the center square after each log is added. Make 10 of block A. The blocks should measure 10½" x 10½".

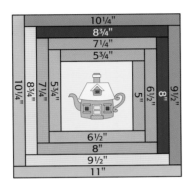

Block A
Make 10.

4. Lay out one embellished square and the log strips for block B as shown. Refer to step 3 to stitch the logs to the embellished square, working counterclockwise. Make 10 of block B. The blocks should measure 10½" x 10½".

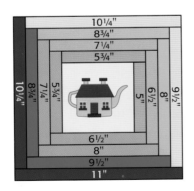

Block B
Make 10.

ASSEMBLING THE QUILT TOP

1. Refer to the quilt assembly diagram to arrange blocks A and B into five rows of four blocks each, alternating the blocks in each row as shown. Stitch the blocks in each row together, and then stitch the rows together.

2. Refer to "Adding Borders" on page 71 to cut the 1½" x 42" light green strips to the correct lengths and stitch them to the quilt top. Repeat with the 3" x 42" coral strips.

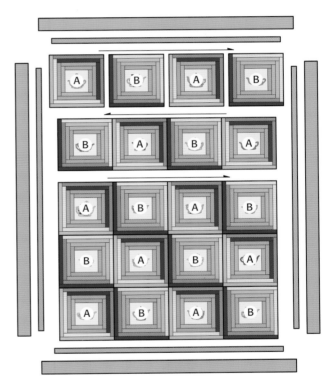

Quilt Assembly Diagram

FINISHING

REFER TO "Quilt Finishing" on pages 71–75.

1. Layer the quilt top with batting and backing; baste.

2. Quilt as desired. The log cabin strips on the featured quilt were stipple stitched throughout the quilt top. The embellished squares of each block are quilted with a gentle arc on each side. The inner border contains a vine design; the outer border is quilted with an overlapping half circle.

3. Trim the backing and batting even with the quilt top.

4. Bind the quilt with the 2½" x 42" light green strips.

5. Add a label.

Alternative Block
Appliqué Pattern

FLORAL WREATH

By Jennifer Lokey, 33¾" x 33¾". Quilted by Allison Bayer.

This elegant, digitized floral wreath took my breath away. The pattern arrangement, as well as the dimensional quality of the finished sewn design, were amazing. And to think I could duplicate this lovely design on my home sewing-and-embroidery machine. A dramatic presentation was called for, so I chose a black background to set off the vibrant thread selection for the embroidered blocks, and I added two coordinating fabrics with subtle prints for the framework.

MATERIALS

Yardage is based on 42"-wide fabric.

For the machine-embroidered project:
- 2⅛ yards of black solid for blocks, border, and binding
- ⅞ yard of coral print for blocks and border
- ⅝ yard of green print for blocks and border
- 1¼ yards of fabric for backing
- 38" x 38" piece of black batting
- Digitized embroidery design of your choice that stitches out to approximately 5" x 5". The floral wreath design used in the featured quilt is by Zundt Design, Number 202134.
- Black tear-away stabilizer
- Sulky 40-weight rayon embroidery threads: Dark Peach (1020), Yellow (1023), Medium Blue (1029), Lemon Yellow (1067), Ecru (1082), Yellow Orange (1137), Avocado (1177), Light Purple (1194)

For the alternative appliquéd design:
- You will need the fabrics and batting listed for the embroidered project, as well as the following:
- ½ yard extra of coral print for appliqués and yo-yos
- ⅛ yard extra of green print for yo-yos

APPLIQUÉ ALTERNATIVE

The pattern for an appliquéd flower with hand-embroidered tendrils and a yo-yo center is given as an alternative to the digitized design.

- 2 skeins of DMC Chili Red (349) 6-strand embroidery floss for finishing appliqué edges (optional)
- 2 skeins of DMC Lime Green (704) 6-strand embroidery floss
- Quilting thread
- Hand-sewing needle
- Hand-embroidery needle
- Freezer paper or fusible web, depending on the appliqué method used

CUTTING

All measurements include ¼"-wide seam allowances.

From the black solid, cut:
- 3 strips, 12" x 42"; crosscut the strips into 12 rectangles, 10" x 12"
- 3 strips, 1¾" x 42"; crosscut the strips into 64 squares, 1¾" x 1¾"
- 1 rectangle, 13" x 30"
- 4 strips, 2½" x 42"

From the coral print, cut:
- 6 strips, 1¾" x 42"; crosscut 3 strips into 48 squares, 1¾" x 1¾"
- 1 rectangle, 13" x 30"

From the green print, cut:
- 10 strips, 1¾" x 42"; crosscut 6 strips into:
    - 52 squares, 1¾" x 1¾"
    - 8 strips, 1¾" x 8"
    - 4 strips, 1¾" x 9¼"

MAKING THE BLOCKS

1. To make the embellished blocks, machine embroider or appliqué each 10" x 12" black rectangle with the chosen design. If you choose to machine embroider, refer to "Machine-Embroidery Basics" on page 9.

   If you choose to appliqué, refer to "Appliqué Basics" on page 11 to prepare and cut 12 flower appliqués from the remaining coral fabric, using the pattern on page 69. Trace the tendril lines onto each block and stemstitch with the lime green embroidery floss. Refer to "Yo-Yo Embellishment" on page 12 to make 96 yo-yos from the remaining coral fabric and 12 yo-yos from the remaining green fabric, using the pattern on page 69. Tack a green yo-yo to the center of each flower appliqué. Tack the coral yo-yos in place between the tendrils where indicated.

2. Refer to "Trimming the Embellished Pieces" on page 15 to trim each embellished rectangle to 6¾" x 6¾".

3. Draw a diagonal line on the wrong side of 48 coral 1¾" x 1¾" squares. Place a marked square in each corner of each embellished square, right sides together. Sew on the marked line; trim ¼" from the stitching line and press the seams toward the center of the block. Make 12 embellished blocks. The blocks should measure 6¾" x 6¾".

Make 12.

4. To make the alternate pieced blocks, stitch the green and coral 1¾" x 42" strips into strip sets A and B as shown. Make two of strip set A and one of strip set B. The strip sets should measure 4¼" wide when sewn. Crosscut the A strip sets into 26 segments, 1¾" wide. Crosscut strip set B into 13 segments, 1¾" wide.

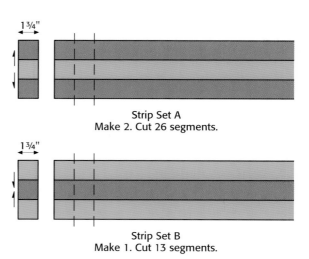

1¾"

Strip Set A
Make 2. Cut 26 segments.

1¾"

Strip Set B
Make 1. Cut 13 segments.

5. Stitch two segments from strip set A and one segment from strip set B together as shown. Make 13 units.

Make 13.

6. To make the half-square-triangle units for the pieced blocks, use a pencil or water-soluble marker to draw a grid of five rows of twelve 2⅛" squares *each* on the wrong side of the 13" x 30" coral rectangle, leaving no space between the squares and rows as shown. Draw a diagonal line through each square. Place the marked rectangle right sides together with the 13" x 30" black rectangle. Pin the layers together between the diagonal lines. Sew ¼" from both sides of each diagonal line.

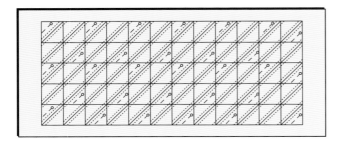

7. Cut along each diagonal, vertical, and horizontal line. This will yield 120 half-square-triangle units. Open each unit and press the seam toward the black fabric. Cut away the extended corners.

Make 120.

8. Sew a half-square-triangle unit to opposite sides of 60 black 1¾" squares as shown. Set aside eight units for the borders.

Make 60.

9. Arrange one unit from step 5, four units from step 8, and four green squares into three horizontal rows as shown. Stitch the pieces in each row together, and then stitch the rows together to complete the pieced block. Make 13 pieced blocks. The blocks should measure 6¾" x 6¾".

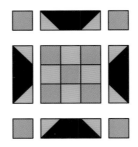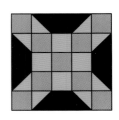

Make 13.

ASSEMBLING THE QUILT TOP

1. To make the pieced borders, stitch together one 1¾" x 9¼" green strip, two 1¾" x 8" green strips, and two of the reserved border units from step 8 of "Making the Blocks" as shown. Make four pieced borders.

1¾" x 8"   1¾" x 9¼"   1¾" x 8"

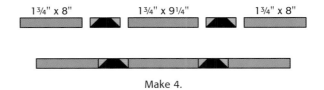

Make 4.

2. Refer to the quilt assembly diagram to arrange the embellished blocks and alternate pieced blocks into five horizontal rows of five blocks each, alternating the position of the blocks in each row as shown. Stitch the blocks in each row together, and then stitch the rows together to complete the center design area.

3. Stitch a pieced border strip from step 1 to the sides of the quilt top as shown in the quilt assembly diagram. Sew a 1¾" black square to each end of the two remaining border strips; stitch the strips to the top and bottom edges of the quilt top.

Quilt Assembly Diagram

FINISHING

Refer to "Quilt Finishing" on pages 71–75.

1. Layer the quilt top with batting and backing; baste.

2. Quilt as desired. A circle was stitched around the wreath of the embellished blocks in the quilt featured. The black fabric outside of the circle was then stipple stitched. The pieced diagonal rows feature three rows of straight lines through the center portion. A subtle arc was quilted in the nine-patch portion of the pieced blocks and through the green border strips.

3. Trim the backing and batting even with the quilt top.

4. Bind the quilt with the 2½" x 42" black strips.

5. Add a label.

Yo-yo placement

Flower

Yo-Yo

**Alternative Block
Appliqué, Yo-Yo, and Hand-Embroidery Patterns**

QUILT FINISHING

*A*FTER THE QUILT center design is stitched together, it's time to add borders, layer with batting and backing, quilt, and bind. Instructions for making a creative label also can be found in this section.

ADDING BORDERS

THE QUILTS in this book feature straight-cut or pieced borders. Most of the straight-cut borders call for strips to be cut the width of the fabric. In some cases the border lengths are longer than the 42" width of the fabric and require the border strips to be pieced together. To do this, you sew the strips end to end and then trim to the measured border length.

Straight-Cut Borders

1. To determine the length of the side borders, measure the quilt top through the vertical center. Cut two border strips to this measurement, piecing and trimming strips when needed to attain the required length.

2. Pin-mark the center of the border strips and the sides of the quilt top.

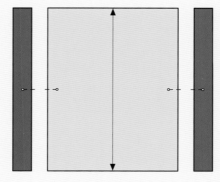

Measure center of quilt, top to bottom. Mark centers.

3. With right sides together, pin the border strips to the quilt top, matching center pins and ends. Stitch the borders to the quilt top. Press the seams toward the borders.

4. To determine the length of the top and bottom borders, measure the quilt top through the horizontal center. Cut two border strips to this measurement, piecing and trimming strips when needed to attain the required length. Mark the centers of the border strips and quilt top.

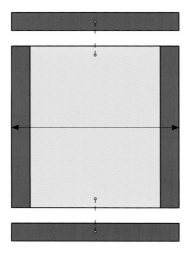

Measure center of quilt, side to side, including borders. Mark centers.

5. With right sides together, pin the border strips to the top and bottom of the quilt top, matching center points and ends. Stitch the borders to the quilt top. Press the seams toward the borders.

LAYERING AND BASTING

THE BACKING should be pieced when necessary, and then cut to measure 2" larger that the quilt top on all sides. Cut the batting to the same size as the backing.

1. Press the backing, and then lay it out on a flat surface, wrong side up. Gently smooth out the fabric to eliminate any fullness. Tape the backing to the work surface, beginning at the center points of the outer edge, then taping down the four corners and along the sides. Keep the backing as straight and square as possible.

2. Place the batting on top of the backing and gently smooth out any creases or folds. Tape the batting to the work surface, matching the straight edges of the backing.

3. Do a final pressing of the quilt top from the back to set the seams in the correct direction. Place the quilt top, right side up, onto the batting, matching the center points of the quilt sides with the tape pieces that are marking the center points of the backing and batting.

Thread Basting for Hand Quilting

Baste the layers with a needle and contrasting color thread. Begin in the center of the quilt and work out to each corner, returning to the center each time. Continue to baste from the center to the outer edges to form a grid of parallel lines 6" to 8" apart. Finally, baste a row of stitches around the outside edges. Remove the pins and you are ready to quilt.

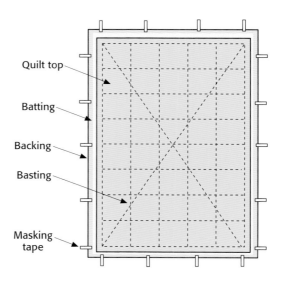

Quilt top

Batting

Backing

Basting

Masking tape

Pin Basting for Machine Quilting

Place #2 safety pins approximately 3" to 4" apart throughout the entire quilt. Begin pinning in the center of the quilt and gently smooth the quilt as you work out toward the edges. Be careful not to place the pins where you intend to stitch. Finally, pin around the outside edges.

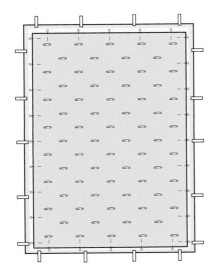

QUILTING

ONCE THE layers are basted together, it's time to secure them with quilting. Whether you choose to machine or hand quilt is entirely up to you.

Hand Quilting

1. Hand quilting may be done on a frame, large hoop, or in your lap. Use one strand of quilting thread and make a small knot in the end. Insert the needle through the top and batting of your project about ¾" from where you want to begin quilting and bring the needle up on the quilting line. Give the thread a sharp tug so that the knot pops below the surface of the quilt top and buries itself in the batting.

2. Using a thimble on the middle finger of your sewing hand, guide your needle straight down so that the point makes gentle contact with the finger below. Direct the needle back to the surface and pull the thread through.

3. Work evenly spaced running stitches through all three layers. As you become more proficient, "load" the needle with several stitches at one time before pulling the thread through.

4. To end stitching, wind the thread twice around the needle. Insert the needle through the quilt top and batting only and then bring it back up through the top. Pull the needle away from the previous quilting line and tug the thread to bury the knot beneath the surface. Hold the thread taut and clip it close to the quilt.

5. When the quilting is complete, trim the batting and backing even with the quilt top to be sure all of the edges are straight and the corners are square.

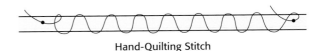

Hand-Quilting Stitch

Machine Quilting

Because my love is designing and playing with fabric as opposed to the actual quilting, all of my quilts are machine quilted either on a home sewing machine or a long-arm quilting machine. The variety of continuous-line quilting designs available today for the home machine quilter creates endless design options. Custom designs by professional long-arm quilters also can enhance and highlight every aspect of your quilt project.

To machine quilt on your home sewing machine, it is helpful to use a walking foot to feed the quilt layers through the machine. A walking foot helps you avoid puckers or wrinkles and is perfect for straight line and in-the-ditch (along the seam line) quilting. Use a darning foot with the machine's feed dogs dropped for free-motion quilting so that you can guide the fabric for outline, stippling, or curved designs.

When the quilting is complete, trim the batting and backing even with the quilt top and be sure all of the edges are straight and the corners are square.

BINDING

DOUBLE-FOLD, straight-grain binding is used to finish the quilts in this book. Cut the binding strips across the width of the fabric. Cutting measurements are given in the individual project instructions.

1. Join the binding strips together to make one continuous strip. To join the strips, place the ends of the binding strips at right angles as shown, right sides together, and stitch across the diagonal of the intersection. Trim the seam to ¼"; press the seams open.

2. Cut one end of the binding strip at a 45° angle, and then turn and press the end under ¼". Press the strip in half lengthwise, wrong sides together.

3. Place the angled end of the binding 8" from the corner on one side of the quilt. Starting 4" from the corner, stitch the binding to the quilt with a ¼" seam allowance. Stop stitching ¼" from the corner of the quilt and backstitch.

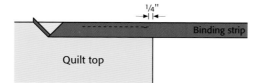

4. Turn the quilt 90°. Fold the binding up and away from the quilt, and then back down onto itself. Align the raw edges of the binding with the quilt-top edge and stitch the binding to the next side of the quilt, stopping ¼" from the next corner. Continue this process around the remainder of the quilt and stop within 4" of the starting point.

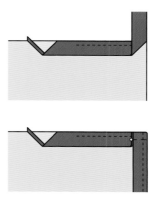

5. Lay the remainder of the binding over the starting point. Leave 1" overlapping the starting point and cut away any excess binding, cutting the end at a 45° angle. Tuck the end into the starting point fold and finish sewing the binding to the quilt.

6. Fold the binding over the quilt edges to the quilt back so that the fold of the binding just covers the row of machine stitching. Blind stitch the binding and mitered corners in place.

CREATIVE QUILT LABELS

MACHINE EMBROIDERY offers a creative opportunity to make a decorative addition to your signature on the back of your quilt. The embroidered design featured in the quilt top may be a perfect focus for your label. To make a label, follow these steps:

1. Cut the label fabric piece large enough to embroider the design and add your message, with plenty of room left to decide the finished label size when your signature is complete.

2. Hoop the label fabric close to the left side of the fabric piece. Stitch out your chosen design.

3. Using a fine-point fabric marking pen, simply write the phrase directly onto the label, or create the message on the computer in a font and size that is legible, such as 20-point, and print the message onto paper. Then, position the fabric over the words, secure it with tape, and trace the message onto the label.

4. Determine the finished label size, add ¼" on all sides, and cut the label to your measured size. Cut a backing piece the exact size as your cut label.

5. With right sides together, stitch the label to the backing piece, using a ¼" seam allowance, and leaving a 2" to 3" opening for turning.

6. Turn the label right side out, press, and hand stitch the opening closed. Your label is ready to sew onto your quilt back.

RESOURCES

𝒯HE FOLLOWING RESOURCES sell digitized machine-embroidery designs.

Amazing Designs
888-874-6760
www.amazingdesigns.com

Cactus Punch, Inc.
4955 N. Shamrock Place
Tucson, AZ 85705
800-487-6972
www.cactuspunch.com

Jennifer Lokey Design Studio
910 Vinecrest Lane
Richardson, TX 75080
972-783-7661
www.jenniferlokey.com

Oklahoma Embroidery Supply and Design (OESD, Inc.)
12101 I-35 Service Road
Oklahoma City, OK 73131
800-580-8885
www.embroideryonline.com

Zundt Design Ltd.
888-533-7397
www.zundtdesign.com

ABOUT THE AUTHOR

$\mathcal{T}$HROUGHOUT JENNIFER LOKEY'S childhood years, she watched her grandmother, Dolly, her mother, Ellie, and her aunt, Mary Jane, sew garments, repair bath towels, do constant mending, and make quilts. Not until after she was grown, married, and her youngest was in school did Jennifer realize there was an imprint on her heart and in her imagination from the loving women in her life.

Once her three boys were in school and she had time for herself, Jennifer began to learn as much as possible about the art of quiltmaking. The fabrics, threads, tools, and techniques were all fascinating to her, and she began an adventure that continues to today.

In 1986, Jennifer cofounded a quilt pattern company, Four Corners Designs, with Remona Stoker. After 15 years as president, Jennifer made the decision to venture out on her own to consider new and innovative design ideas to share with her quilter friends. Thus this book, using machine embroidery to enhance beautiful quilts, was conceived.

Jennifer and her husband, Fred, reside in Richardson, Texas, where they have lived for the past 26 years. Their home is within walking distance of their three sons and their spouses and children, who are all a constant delight.

new and bestselling titles from

Martingale® & COMPANY

America's Best-Loved Craft & Hobby Books®

That Patchwork Place®

America's Best-Loved Quilt Books®

NEW RELEASES
20 Decorated Baskets
Asian Elegance
Batiks and Beyond
Classic Knitted Vests
Clever Quilts Encore
Crocheted Socks!
Four Seasons of Quilts
Happy Endings
Judy Murrah's Jacket Jackpot
Knits for Children and Their Teddies
Loving Stitches
Meadowbrook Quilts
Once More around the Block
Pairing Up
Patchwork Memories
Pretty and Posh
Professional Machine Quilting
Purely Primitive
Shadow Appliqué
Snowflake Follies
Style at Large
Trashformations
World of Quilts, A

APPLIQUÉ
Appliquilt in the Cabin
Artful Album Quilts
Blossoms in Winter
Color-Blend Appliqué
Garden Party
Sunbonnet Sue All through the Year

HOLIDAY QUILTS & CRAFTS
Christmas Cats and Dogs
Christmas Delights
Creepy Crafty Halloween
Handcrafted Christmas, A
Hocus Pocus!
Make Room for Christmas Quilts
Snowman's Family Album Quilt, A
Welcome to the North Pole

LEARNING TO QUILT
101 Fabulous Rotary-Cut Quilts
Casual Quilter, The
Fat Quarter Quilts
More Fat Quarter Quilts
Quick Watercolor Quilts
Quilts from Aunt Amy
Simple Joys of Quilting, The
Your First Quilt Book (or it should be!)

PAPER PIECING
40 Bright and Bold Paper-Pieced Blocks
50 Fabulous Paper-Pieced Stars
Down in the Valley
Easy Machine Paper Piecing
For the Birds
It's Raining Cats and Dogs
Papers for Foundation Piecing
Quilter's Ark, A
Show Me How to Paper Piece
Traditional Quilts to Paper Piece

QUILTS FOR BABIES & CHILDREN
Easy Paper-Pieced Baby Quilts
Even More Quilts for Baby
More Quilts for Baby
Play Quilts
Quilts for Baby
Sweet and Simple Baby Quilts

ROTARY CUTTING/SPEED PIECING
101 Fabulous Rotary-Cut Quilts
365 Quilt Blocks a Year Perpetual Calendar
1000 Great Quilt Blocks
Around the Block Again
Around the Block with Judy Hopkins
Cutting Corners
Log Cabin Fever
Pairing Up
Strips and Strings
Triangle-Free Quilts
Triangle Tricks

SCRAP QUILTS
Nickel Quilts
Rich Traditions
Scrap Frenzy
Spectacular Scraps
Successful Scrap Quilts

TOPICS IN QUILTMAKING
Americana Quilts
Bed and Breakfast Quilts
Bright Quilts from Down Under
Creative Machine Stitching
Everyday Embellishments
Fabulous Quilts from Favorite Patterns
Folk Art Friends
Handprint Quilts
Just Can't Cut It!
Quilter's Home: Winter, The
Split-Diamond Dazzlers
Time to Quilt

CRAFTS
300 Papermaking Recipes
ABCs of Making Teddy Bears, The
Blissful Bath, The
Creating with Paint
Handcrafted Frames
Handcrafted Garden Accents
Painted Whimsies
Pretty and Posh
Sassy Cats
Stamp in Color

KNITTING & CROCHET
365 Knitting Stitches a Year
    Perpetual Calendar
Basically Brilliant Knits
Crochet for Tots
Crocheted Aran Sweaters
Knitted Sweaters for Every Season
Knitted Throws and More
Knitter's Template, A
Knitting with Novelty Yarns
More Paintbox Knits
Simply Beautiful Sweaters for Men
Today's Crochet
Too Cute! Cotton Knits for Toddlers
Treasury of Rowan Knits, A
Ultimate Knitter's Guide, The

Our books are available at bookstores and your favorite craft, fabric, and yarn retailers. If you don't see the title you're looking for, visit us at **www.martingale-pub.com** or contact us at:

1-800-426-3126

International: 1-425-483-3313 • Fax: 1-425-486-7596 • Email: info@martingale-pub.com

For more information and a full list of our titles, visit our Web site.